Miss Grimble Presents
Delicious Desserts

Miss Grimble Presents
Delicious Desserts

Sylvia Balser Hirsch

MACMILLAN PUBLISHING COMPANY
New York
COLLIER MACMILLAN PUBLISHERS
London

Macmillan Publishing Company
866 Third Avenue, New York, N.Y. 10022
Collier Macmillan Canada, Inc.

Library of Congress Cataloging in Publication Data
Hirsch, Sylvia Balser.
Miss Grimble presents delicious desserts.
Includes index.
1. Desserts.   I. Title.
TX773.H55   1983   641.8′6   83-5394
ISBN 0-02-551860-7

Printed in the United States of America

Dedicated to the hungriest,
most appreciative people
in the world—my family!

Contents

Introduction

Ever since my seventh-grade home economics teacher voted me "the girl least likely to be a good homemaker," I have been determined to prove her wrong. This determination was a bit latent, I admit, for it wasn't until I married and had to phone Mother long distance for instructions on making coffee that I decided to open a cookbook and learn the mysteries of the kitchen.

And mysteries they were, too. My first attempt at the tried and true "bride's first dinner"—steak, baked potato, and salad—was a fiasco! The potatoes exploded in the oven for lack of prebake piercing and the steaks were crisp, *but* the coffee was good.

I always liked to read, and so I began to read cookbooks—not just recipes, but the instructions to many of our gustatory delights, the whys and wherefores of culinary expertise. I am not now and have never been a professional baker. All of my attempts have been made to please my family and friends and conquer my childhood fear of the kitchen.

For nearly forty years I have been collecting recipes from family and friends and gracious chefs who willingly parted with heirloom secrets. During our travels here and abroad, I hunted through old bookstores for "antique" cookbooks containing gems of the past, most of which had to be reworked from a teacup and a handful to the acceptable legal measures of today.

This book is really a compilation of years of trial and error. The Grimble Cheesecake, as it is sold in our bakery, is the original dating back nearly forty years. It was one of my first successes and has always been a favorite for home and parties.

In baking a cheesecake, for which I am best known—to quote *McCall's* magazine—"Miss Grimble Is the My Fair Lady of the Cheesecake World"—the varieties are endless and you and I are limited only by our own imaginations.

Since opening the bakery, we have received letters from housewives all over the country, offering their prized family recipes for cheesecake. That is tantamount to praise from Mount Olympus!

As one cheesecake "maven" to another—enjoy!

Dos and Don'ts

Do have all ingredients at room temperature.

Don't beat egg whites in an electric mixer, *unless* instructions say otherwise.

Do beat egg whites on a large platter with a flat type wire whisk. This assures the maximum volume of whites owing to the open area of the platter. Your desserts will always be lighter, larger, and fluffier. This rule applies to all cakes and soufflés.

Do preheat the oven at least 10 to 15 minutes before baking.

Do use an oven thermometer; thermostats vary widely.

If cheesecakes brown too quickly at designated oven temperatures, cover top loosely with foil for the duration of the baking.

Do, when baking a chocolate or mocha cake, dust the pan with cocoa.

Do, by all means, experiment with flavors and crusts.

Cheesecakes and Cheese Desserts

Classic Crumb Crust
Chocolate Coconut Crust
Suggested Variations for Cheesecakes
ABC Cheesecake
My Mother's Regal Cheesecake
Famous Hanan Cheesecake
"Almost" Lindy's Cheesecake
Velvet Cheesecake
Macaroon Rum Raisin Cheesecake
Coffee Rum Cheesecake
Cointreau Cheesecake
Caramel Pecan Cheesecake
Unique Roquefort Marvel
Refrigerator Loaf Cheesecake
Austrian Cheese Torte
Italian Molded Refrigerator Cheesecake

§   CHOCOLATE CHEESECAKES   §
Chocolate Cheesecake
Chocolate Walnut Cheesecake
Chocolate Cheese Crown
Chocolate-Glazed Cheese Torte
Chocolate Orange Marbled Cheesecake
Mocha Cheesecake

(Continued)

§ CHEESE DESSERTS §

Italian Cheese Soufflé
Coconut Lemon Cheese Pie
Coeur à la Crème
Cheese Delights
Macaroon Cheese Whip

Classic Crumb Crust for a 9-Inch Pie Shell

1½ cups crumbs—vanilla or chocolate wafers, graham crackers, gingersnaps, or zwieback

4 tablespoons butter, melted

2 tablespoons sugar

Blend all ingredients well and press onto the bottom and up the sides of the pan called for in the recipe.

Preheated crusts are crisper. If a crumb crust is to be baked before filling, bake it at 300° for 15 minutes and thoroughly cool. If the crust is not to be baked first, it must be thoroughly chilled.

VARIATIONS:

Chocolate–Add 2 tablespoons melted bitter chocolate.

Coconut–Substitute ⅓ cup flaked coconut for ⅓ cup crumbs.

Mocha–Add 1½ tablespoons cocoa and 1 teaspoon instant powdered coffee.

Nut–Add finely chopped almonds, pecans, walnuts, or pignoli nuts, and decrease crumbs by an equal amount.

Orange–Add 2 tablespoons grated orange zest.

Orange-Chocolate–Add 2 tablespoons grated orange zest and 2 tablespoons melted bitter chocolate. Do not bake.

Spiced crust–Add ½ teaspoon cinnamon and ½ teaspoon ground ginger, or ½ teaspoon cinnamon and ¼ teaspoon cloves or allspice.

Spiced lemon–Add 1 teaspoon cinnamon and 1 teaspoon grated lemon zest.

Any of the above crusts are easily adapted for cheesecake bases by merely doubling the recipe. This will be sufficient for 9″ or 10″ springform pans.

Chocolate Coconut Crust

This versatile crust lends itself to so many fillings. To suggest a few: vanilla or strawberry ice cream, mocha or chocolate mousse, or cold Bavarian cream.

9" pie pan, buttered
2 tablespoons butter
2 ounces bitter chocolate
⅔ cup confectioners' sugar, sifted
2 tablespoons hot milk
1½ cups unsweetened shredded coconut

Combine butter and chocolate in top of double boiler over hot water and stir until chocolate is melted. Combine the sugar with the milk, stir well, then stir into the chocolate mixture. Remove from heat and fold in the shredded coconut. Spoon the mixture into the buttered pan and press firmly on the bottom and up the sides. Refrigerate until firm.

Fill with 3–3½ cups softened ice cream or sherbet, or Bavarian cream, or other filling. WITH A FILLING, SERVES 8.

Suggested Variations for Cheesecakes

All pans for crumb crusts should be buttered so the crumbs adhere better. Sprinkle crumb crust with 1 tablespoon brandy.

Substitute brown sugar for white or blend half and half.

Add chopped maraschino cherries, chopped glazed fruits, citron, or raisins to the bottom of crust before the filling or blend into filling.

Cover the bottom of the crumb-lined pan with well-drained crushed pineapple, very thick fruit preserves, thin apple slices, or extra-thick applesauce. For this variation, the bottom of the crust should be extra thick to prevent fruit from seeping through and causing crust to stick to the pan.

Top any cheesecake with fresh fruit—plain or crushed with sugar and a dash of lemon or orange juice.

CHEESECAKES

The ABC Cheesecake

This is as simple as a cheesecake can be. For a beginner, it's perfect.

9" springform, buttered

CRUST:
16 *honey graham crackers,*
  crushed (equals 2 cups)
4 *tablespoons butter, melted*

Combine the crumbs and butter and line the bottom and sides of the springform.

FILLING:
3 *8-ounce packages cream*
  cheese
1 *cup sugar*
4 *eggs, separated*
1 *teaspoon vanilla*

Preheat oven to 350°F.

In an electric mixer, cream the cheese with the sugar, egg yolks, and vanilla until smooth. Beat the egg whites until stiff and gently fold into cheese mixture. Pour into prepared form and bake in preheated oven for 40–50 minutes. Remove from the oven.

TOPPING:
1 *pint sour cream*
2 *tablespoons sugar*
1 *teaspoon vanilla*

Blend ingredients and gently spoon over cake.

Return to the oven and bake for 5 minutes at 475°. (The topping will not have set yet.) Remove cake from oven, cool to room temperature, then refrigerate overnight.
SERVES 10–12.

My Mother's Regal Cheesecake

This was always baked with love and devotion and received in the same way.

9" springform, buttered

CRUST:
1½ cups zwieback crumbs
2 tablespoons butter, melted
2 tablespoons sugar

FILLING:
2 8-ounce packages cream
  cheese
1 cup sugar plus ¼ cup
  reserved
5 eggs, separated
2 cups sour cream
1 teaspoon vanilla
1 teaspoon fresh lemon juice
Whole strawberries or raspberries for garnish

Blend crumbs, butter, and sugar, and line the bottom and sides of the springform.

Preheat oven to 300°F.

In an electric mixer, cream the cheese with 1 cup sugar and the egg yolks and beat thoroughly. Add the sour cream, vanilla, and lemon juice, and blend well. Beat the egg whites with the remaining ¼ cup sugar until stiff and gently fold into cheese mixture. Spoon into shell and bake in preheated oven for 1 hour. Turn off the oven and let the cake remain in the oven for 1 hour with the door closed and then an additional ½ hour with the door open. Chill overnight. Serve with berries and/or a bowl of lightly sweetened sour cream.
SERVES 10–12.

The Famous Hanan Cheesecake

Mr. Hanan, who retired from baking, gave me this recipe. My first little shop had been open about six months and received two reviews in *New York Magazine* and one national review in *McCall's* magazine. The three caught his attention, and he decided I was the one to inherit this divine creation. It cannot be produced commercially as it is far too delicate.

10" springform, buttered

CRUST:
1½ cups honey graham
   cracker crumbs (about 21
   crackers)
3 sticks butter, melted
¾ cup sugar

Combine the crumbs, butter, and sugar, and press onto the bottom and sides of the springform pan.

FILLING:
2 8-ounce and 4 3-ounce
   packages cream cheese
7 eggs, separated
½ cup sugar
2 tablespoons imitation vanilla—must be A&P brand

Preheat oven to 375°F.

Cream the cheese with the egg yolks until smooth. Add the sugar and vanilla. Beat 5 egg whites to a soft peak and gently fold into the cream cheese batter. Pour into prepared spring-form and bake 35–40 minutes. Remove from oven and cool 1 hour.

TOPPING:
2 cups sour cream
3 tablespoons sugar
2 tablespoons imitation vanilla

Beat sour cream with sugar and vanilla until blended. Spread gently and evenly over the top of the cake and return to oven for 6 minutes. Remove from oven and cool to room temperature and then refrigerate. Before serving, top with lightly salted, slivered toasted almonds and dust with powdered sugar.
SERVES 12–16.

"Almost" Lindy's Cheesecake

The following recipe was sent to me many years ago as the authentic Lindy's famous cheesecake. Whether it is or not is up to those who had the distinct pleasure of eating at Lindy's during its heyday to judge. For what it's worth, nostalgically speaking, here's Lindy's famous cheesecake.

9" springform, buttered

CRUST:
1 cup all-purpose flour
¼ cup sugar
1 teaspoon grated lemon zest
¼ teaspoon vanilla
1 egg yolk
1 stick butter
ice water, if necessary

Preheat oven to 400°F.

Prepare dough by combining flour, sugar, lemon zest, and vanilla. Make a well in the center and add the egg yolk and butter. Work together quickly with pastry blender or hands. Add 1–2 tablespoons ice water if necessary to bind dough. Wrap dough in waxed paper and chill thoroughly, at least one hour.

Remove ring from springform. Roll one-third of the dough ⅛" thick and place over bottom of pan. Trim the edge and bake in preheated oven 12–15 minutes until a light golden brown. Cool. Place the springform sides over the baked base. Roll the remaining dough ⅛ inch thick and cut to fit the sides of the pan, pressing firmly to fit and seal the base. Trim the dough to come only ¾ up the sides.

FILLING:
5 8-ounce packages cream cheese
1¾ cups sugar
3 tablespoons all-purpose flour
5 eggs
2 egg yolks
1½ teaspoons lemon zest
1½ teaspoons orange zest
½ teaspoon vanilla
¼ cup heavy cream

Turn oven up to 550°F.

Cream cheese with sugar and flour until smooth. Add eggs and two additional yolks one at a time and blend. Add the flavorings and cream, mix well, and pour into prepared springform. Bake at 550°F for 10–12 minutes, then reduce temperature to 200°F and continue to bake for 1 hour. Cool the cake to room temperature before glazing or serving.

STRAWBERRY GLAZE:
1 quart strawberries, washed, hulled, and drained
2 teaspoons cornstarch
¼ cup water
¾ cup sugar
Pinch salt
1 teaspoon butter

Cover top of cooled cake with select firm strawberries. Crush about 1 cup of remaining strawberries and put in a saucepan. Dissolve the cornstarch in the water, then add to the saucepan with sugar and salt. Boil gently for about 2 minutes, stirring constantly. Remove from heat and stir in butter. Cool, then spoon over berry-topped cake.
SERVES 12.

Velvet Cheesecake

8" springform, buttered

CRUST:
1 cup zwieback, crushed
   (about 12 cookies)
4 tablespoons butter, melted
¼ cup extra fine sugar
1 teaspoon grated lemon zest

Combine crumbs, melted butter, extra fine sugar, and 1 teaspoon of the lemon zest. Press mixture onto bottom and sides of pan, reserving ¼ cup.

FILLING:
2 teaspoons grated lemon zest
1¼ pounds creamed cottage cheese
1 cup granulated sugar
1½ tablespoons all-purpose flour
1 teaspoon grated orange zest
¼ teaspoon vanilla
3 eggs
1 egg yolk
2 tablespoons heavy cream

Preheat oven to 250°F.
   Combine 2 teaspoons lemon zest, cheese, sugar, flour, orange zest, and vanilla. Beat thoroughly until fluffy. Beat in one egg at a time, then the egg yolk and cream. Spoon into prepared pan and sprinkle with reserved crumbs. Bake in preheated oven for 1 hour. Turn off the heat; leave the cheesecake in the closed oven for 1 hour. Remove from oven, and let cool slowly at room temperature. Chill before serving.
SERVES 8–10.

Macaroon Rum Raisin Cheesecake

I think there is evidence of the fine Italian hand here. It's delicious.

9" springform, buttered

CRUST:
*2 cups crumbled almond
  macaroons*

Press the macaroon crumbs onto the bottom and sides of the springform, reserving some for top.

FILLING:
*½ cup golden raisins
⅓ cup dark Jamaica rum
1 pound ricotta cheese, sieved
5 eggs, separated
½ cup sugar
1 teaspoon lemon juice
1 teaspoon vanilla
Pinch salt*

Preheat oven to 300°F.

Soak raisins in rum and set aside. Combine cheese, egg yolks, and sugar in an electric mixer and blend thoroughly. Add lemon juice, vanilla, and salt. Now add the raisins with the rum.

Beat egg whites until stiff and gently fold into cheese mixture. Pour into prepared pan, dust top with reserved crumbs, and bake in preheated oven for about 1 hour. Turn off heat and leave cake in oven with the door closed for 2 hours. Remove from oven and chill overnight before serving.
SERVES 8–10.

VARIATION:
Coconut macaroon crumbs may be substituted for the bottom only.

Coffee Rum Cheesecake

This unusual combination of flavors is quite unique.

*9" pie shell or chocolate crumb
  crust, baked and cooled
4 3-ounce packages cream
  cheese, softened
1 cup sugar*

In an electric mixer blend the cheese, sugar, coffee, rum, and zest until creamy. Dissolve gelatin in hot water and blend into cheese mixture. Whip the cream until stiff and gently fold into mixture. Blend well and spoon into prepared

2 tablespoons extra-strong
    coffee or espresso
2 tablespoons light rum
1 teaspoon grated lemon zest
1 tablespoon unflavored
    gelatin
2 tablespoons hot water
1 cup heavy cream
Additional whipped cream for
    garnish

shell. Chill several hours before serving. Decorate with additional whipped cream.
SERVES 6–8.

Cointreau Cheesecake

Many years ago this recipe appeared in a tiny booklet tied around the neck of a bottle of Cointreau. Thanks to their ingenuity, this is a perfect party dessert for the sophisticated palate!

9" springform, buttered

CRUST:

Use the Classic Crumb Crust recipe (p. 3) with honey graham crackers or zwieback, bake and then cool.

FILLING:
1 pound pot cheese, sieved
1 8-ounce package cream
    cheese
1 cup sugar
¼ cup all-purpose flour
½ teaspoon salt
4 eggs, separated
1 teaspoon grated lemon zest
½ cup Cointreau
½ cup heavy cream, whipped

Preheat oven to 325°F.
    Combine the two cheeses in an electric mixer and beat until smooth and fluffy. Sift sugar, flour, and salt together and add to the mixture, blending thoroughly. Add egg yolks and mix again. Stir in the zest, Cointreau, and whipped cream. Beat egg whites until stiff and fold into the batter. Pour into prepared shell and bake in preheated oven for 1 hour and 15 minutes. Turn off the heat and leave in the oven with the door closed for 1 hour. Remove, cool to room temperature then chill 3–4 hours before serving.
SERVES 8–10.

Caramel Pecan Cheesecake

Another lovely creation of the Grimble bakery that became too expensive to produce commercially.

10" springform, buttered

CRUST:
2 cups honey graham cracker
   crumbs
2 tablespoons sugar
6 tablespoons butter or
   margarine, melted

Blend the crumbs with the sugar and shortening. Press onto the bottom and sides of the springform.

FILLING:
3 8-ounce packages cream
   cheese
4 eggs
2 cups dark brown sugar,
   packed
1½ teaspoons instant
   powdered coffee
1 tablespoon vanilla
⅛ teaspoon salt
½ cup chopped pecans
Chopped pecans for garnish
Butter

Preheat oven to 350°F.

In an electric mixer, cream the cheese with the eggs and sugar. Add the instant coffee, vanilla, salt, and pecans, and mix on medium speed until well-blended. Pour into prepared springform and bake in preheated oven for 40–45 minutes. Cool to room temperature, then chill. To serve, top with additional chopped pecans that have been lightly tossed in butter.
SERVES 10–12.

The Unique Roquefort Marvel

Just to add interest to this unusual pastry, bear with me long enough to learn a bit about this cheese. Roquefort, as the name implies, comes from Roquefort, France. It is there, for over 2000 years, that this wonderful product of pure sheep's milk has been cured and ripened in caves in the mountains, then shipped around the world for discerning palates. And now, my salute to the French who devised this cheesecake.

9" springform, buttered

CRUST:
1½ cups crushed cornflakes, or any dry, unsweetened, toasted cereal
4 tablespoons butter, melted

Combine cereal and butter and press onto bottom and sides of springform.

FILLING:
4 8-ounce packages cream cheese
6 ounces Roquefort cheese
¼ cup all-purpose flour
1 cup sugar
6 eggs, separated
1 cup sour cream
1½ tablespoons grated lemon zest
Pinch salt
Fresh berries, sliced fresh peaches, or green grapes for garnish

Preheat oven to 325°F.

Combine the two cheeses in an electric mixer and beat until creamy. Mix flour with ½ cup of the sugar and add to the mixture. Now add the egg yolks, sour cream, zest, and salt, and beat until thoroughly mixed. Beat egg whites to a soft peak, adding the other ½ cup sugar gradually, and continue to beat until stiff. Fold gently into the cheesecake batter and pour into prepared pan. Bake in preheated oven for 1 hour, or until center seems firm. Turn off oven heat and allow cake to cool in oven.

Pass fresh berries or fresh sliced peaches—or garnish with the same before serving. I even like to serve seedless green grapes as an interesting accompaniment, for what could be better than grapes and cheese!
SERVES 8–10.

Refrigerator Loaf Cheesecake

An unusual departure from cheesecake preparation—but a winner, nonetheless.

10" × 4" loaf pan, lined with
*   waxed paper*

CRUST:

Use the Classic Crumb Crust recipe (p. 3) with honey graham crackers, adding ¼ teaspoon cinnamon.

FILLING:
1 pound cottage cheese, sieved
3 whole eggs
½ cup sugar
3 tablespoons all-purpose
*   flour*
⅓ cup milk
1 teaspoon grated lemon zest
Pinch salt
1 teaspoon fresh lemon juice
1 cup heavy cream, whipped

Combine the cheese, eggs, sugar, flour, milk, lemon zest, and salt in an electric mixer and beat until creamy. Transfer mixture to top of double boiler and cook over hot water, stirring constantly, until thick. (This will take about 10–15 minutes.) Cool thoroughly, add lemon juice and fold into the whipped cream. Cover the bottom of the lined pan with one-third of the crumbs. Pour in half the cheese mixture, another one-third of the crumbs, remaining cheese mixture and top with last third of crumbs. Refrigerate overnight. Invert on serving platter, remove waxed paper and decorate top with the following:

TOPPING:
1 cup heavy cream
1 tablespoon sugar
1 teaspoon grated orange zest
1 teaspoon grated lemon zest
1 pint fresh strawberries,
*   washed, stemmed, and*
*   dried*

Whip the cream with the sugar. Blend fruit zests into sweetened whipped cream and cover top and sides of cake. Cover the top with strawberries. Slice like any loaf cake.
SERVES 8–10.

Austrian Cheese Torte

This reminds me a great deal of the French Roquefort cheesecake, but the rich butter/nut crust makes this torte quite unusual.

9" springform, buttered

CRUST:
1½ cups all-purpose flour, sifted
⅓ cup sugar
10–11 tablespoons butter
2 egg yolks, beaten
¼ cup finely grated almonds
¼ teaspoon salt

FILLING:
4 ounces cream cheese
2 ounces imported blue cheese, sieved
4 tablespoons butter
6 tablespoons sugar
4 eggs, separated
¼ cup all-purpose flour
¼ cup heavy cream
½ cup golden raisins
¼ teaspoon salt
Fresh raspberries or strawberries for garnish

Preheat oven to 400°F.

Sift flour and sugar together, cut in butter until crumbly, add yolks, then almonds, and salt. When well blended, press one-half on the bottom of the form and bake in preheated oven for 10 minutes. Remove from oven and cool, then line sides of form with reserved crust.

In an electric mixer, combine the two cheeses, butter, sugar, egg yolks, and flour, and beat until smooth and creamy. Add the cream and mix thoroughly. Fold in the raisins.

Beat egg whites with the salt until stiff and gently fold into batter. Pour into prepared shell and bake 20–25 minutes until center is set. Remove to rack to cool to room temperature. Remove form and serve with fresh raspberries or fresh strawberries.

SERVES 8–10.

Italian Molded Refrigerator Cheesecake

With apology to no one, I firmly believe the Italians show more imagination in the varied uses of cheese in their fabulous desserts than any other people. Cheesecakes reach an all-time high in southern Italy. The combinations are endless, as witnessed by the following.

6-cup mold

12 ladyfingers, unfilled variety, split

1½ pounds ricotta cheese

1 cup plus 2 tablespoons extra fine granulated sugar

¼ cup crème de cacao

½ cup candied fruits, diced

Candied fruit for garnish

Line the mold—bottom and sides—with about half of the split ladyfingers, cut side facing in. Reserve the rest for the top.

In an electric mixer, combine the cheese, sugar, and liquor, and beat until well blended. Fold the fruit in gently and spoon into prepared mold. Cover the top with ladyfingers and chill at least 8 hours. To serve, turn out of mold and decorate with additional candied fruit.

SERVES 10.

CHOCOLATE CHEESECAKES

Chocolate Cheesecake

This unusually delicious dessert was first served to me by a very dear friend who is one of Dallas's best bakers. The recipe is a variation of a Viennese chocolate cheese torte.

10" springform, buttered and chilled

CRUST:
2 cups crushed vanilla wafers
  or honey graham crackers
5 tablespoons butter, melted
2 tablespoons granulated
  sugar
1 teaspoon cocoa

Blend well. Press onto bottom and sides of springform.

FILLING:
4 eggs, separated
1 cup plus 6 tablespoons
  granulated sugar
12 ounces semisweet chocolate
½ cup extra-strong black
  coffee
1 teaspoon plus ½ teaspoon
  vanilla
3 8-ounce packages cream
  cheese
1 cup heavy cream, whipped
Shaved bitter chocolate for
  garnish

Preheat oven to 350°F.
  Combine egg yolks with ½ cup of the sugar and beat until light and lemony.
  Melt chocolate in top of double boiler with coffee and 1 teaspoon vanilla. Let cool.
  In an electric mixer, beat the cheese until smooth, add the yolk mixture, blend well, then add the cooled chocolate and coffee. Beat the egg whites with ½ cup of the sugar until stiff, but not dry, and fold into the chocolate cheese mixture. Spoon into prepared shell and bake for 1 hour. Turn off the oven, open oven door and allow cake to cool in oven for 1 hour. Refrigerate an hour before serving. Remove ring from springform and top cake with whipped cream that has been sweetened with 6 tablespoons granulated sugar and ½ teaspoon vanilla. Garnish with bitter chocolate curls.
SERVES 10–12.

VARIATION:
In the crust, substitute chocolate wafers, omit the sugar, and add 2 teaspoons instant coffee.

Chocolate Walnut Cheesecake

8" springform, buttered

CRUST:

Use the Classic Crumb Crust recipe (p. 3) replacing ½ cup crumbs with ½ cup chopped walnuts and adding 2 tablespoons melted bitter chocolate.

FILLING:
*3 8-ounce packages cream
    cheese
4 eggs
1 cup sugar
6 ounces semisweet chocolate
    bits
10–11 tablespoons butter
1 cup sour cream
1½ teaspoons vanilla
Pinch salt
¾ cup walnuts, chopped
Sweetened whipped cream for
    garnish
Grated bitter chocolate for
    garnish*

Preheat oven to 325°F.

In an electric mixer, cream the cheese with the eggs and sugar until smooth. Melt chocolate and butter together, and add to the cheese mixture with the sour cream, vanilla, salt, and walnuts. Blend well and pour into prepared shell and bake in preheated oven for 2 hours. Let cake cool to room temperature, then chill overnight. Garnish with sweetened whipped cream and bitter chocolate curls.
SERVES 8–10.

Chocolate Cheese Crown

This combination of flavors is absolutely ambrosial!

*9" springform
18 plain ladyfingers, split
½ cup fresh orange juice
1 8-ounce package cream
    cheese
½ cup brown sugar, packed
⅛ teaspoon salt
1 cup semisweet chocolate
    bits, melted*

Preheat oven to 375°F.

Place split ladyfingers flat side down on pan and toast for 5 minutes at 375°F. Cool, then brush flat side with orange juice. Arrange on bottom and sides of springform, rounded side facing out.

Cream the cheese, brown sugar, salt, and melted chocolate in an electric mixer. Add egg yolks and vanilla and mix thoroughly. Beat the

3 eggs, separated
1½ teaspoons vanilla
½ cup granulated sugar
1½ cups heavy cream
Sweetened whipped cream for
    garnish
Shaved bitter chocolate for
    garnish

egg whites until foamy and gradually add the granulated sugar, continuing to beat until stiff. Fold into the cheese mixture. Whip the cream until stiff and fold this in last. Spoon into prepared shell and chill at least 5 hours. To serve, remove springform ring and garnish top with extra sweetened whipped cream and shaved bitter chocolate.
SERVES 10.

Chocolate-Glazed Cheese Torte

There is always something new under the sun. This combination is a pleasant surprise.

10" springform, buttered
2 sticks butter
1 cup sugar
10 eggs, separated
½ pound pot cheese, sieved
⅓ cup dried bread crumbs
2 cups almonds, blanched and
    chopped fine (reserve ½
    cup for garnish)
2 tablespoons fresh lemon
    juice
1 tablespoon grated lemon zest
Pinch salt

Preheat oven to 350°F.
    Combine butter and sugar in electric mixer and beat until creamy. Add yolks and continue beating. When smooth, mix in remaining ingredients and lastly fold in the egg whites, stiffly beaten. Pour into buttered springform and bake for 1 hour. Cool to room temperature and ice.

ICING:
2 tablespoons butter, softened
1 cup confectioners' sugar,
    sifted
1 teaspoon vanilla
2 ounces bitter chocolate,
    melted
Light cream or half and half

Cream the butter with the sugar and add the other ingredients. Add only enough cream necessary for spreading. Spread evenly over top and sides of cake. Dust with reserved almonds.
SERVES 12.

Chocolate Orange Marbled Cheesecake

This marbling method is a creation of the Grimble Bakery. Lightly sweetened whipped cream, flavored with Grand Marnier or curaçao, is an excellent garnish.

9" springform, buttered

CRUST:

Use the Classic Crumb Crust recipe (p. 3) adding 2 tablespoons melted bitter chocolate and 1 tablespoon grated orange zest. Press onto bottom and sides of springform pan.

FILLING:
5 8-ounce packages cream
  cheese
1⅔ cups sugar
2½ tablespoons all-purpose
  flour
5 whole eggs
3 egg yolks
2 tablespoons grated orange
  zest
¼ cup heavy cream
3 ounces bitter chocolate,
  melted

Preheat oven to 500°F.

Combine all the ingredients in the order listed, except the chocolate, in an electric mixer and beat until well blended. Divide the batter in half and stir melted chocolate into one half. Pour each half of the batter into a 2-cup measuring cup. Holding the handles together in one hand, pour the two batters into prepared springform in a swirling fashion until all the batter is used. Bake in preheated oven for 10 minutes, then reduce heat to 200° and bake an additional hour, until center is firm. Turn off heat and let cake remain in oven until cool, 2–3 hours. Remove to rack and bring to room temperature before removing the sides and serving.
SERVES 8–10.

Mocha Cheesecake

Delight your family and guests with this unusual dessert. And you can gild this lily by passing a bowl of lightly sweetened whipped cream flavored with Kahlua or crème de cacao when serving.

9" springform, buttered

CRUST:

Use a chocolate crumb crust and add ¼ cup ground almonds or hazelnuts. Press onto bottom and sides of springform.

FILLING:
*3 8-ounce packages cream
   cheese
⅔ cup sugar
3 eggs
½ pound semisweet chocolate
4 tablespoons butter
2 teaspoons instant coffee
2 teaspoons water
1½ teaspoons vanilla
3 cups sour cream*

Preheat oven to 350°F.

   Combine the cheese, sugar, and eggs in an electric mixer and beat until creamy. Melt chocolate with butter and add to mixture. Dissolve instant coffee in water and blend into mixture along with the vanilla. Beat thoroughly. Lastly, beat in the sour cream and pour into prepared shell. Bake in preheated oven for 45 minutes. Cool, then chill overnight.
SERVES 8–10.

CHEESE DESERTS

Italian Cheese Soufflé

2-quart soufflé dish, buttered
8 tablespoons butter
½ cup sugar
4 eggs, separated
1 cup ricotta cheese
2 teaspoons fresh lemon juice
⅓ cup sultana raisins
Grated zest of ½ lemon
1 cup sour cream

Preheat oven to 350°F.

In an electric mixer, beat butter, sugar, and egg yolks. Add the cheese and beat until smooth. Stir in the lemon juice, raisins, zest, and sour cream. Beat egg whites until stiff and gently fold into cheese mixture. Spoon into the prepared soufflé dish, set in pan of hot water ⅓ up the sides of the dish, and bake in preheated oven for 50–60 minutes. This delightful dessert should be served immediately.
SERVES 6.

Coconut Lemon Cheese Pie

The snapper in this luscious dessert is the coconut crust. Be sure to use the crust as a base for any chocolate cheesecake.

9" pie pan, heavily buttered
1½–2 cups shredded un-
    sweetened coconut
4 3-ounce packages cream
    cheese
3 eggs
¾ cup sugar
3 tablespoons fresh lemon
    juice
Grated zest of 1 lemon
1 cup heavy cream
1 tablespoon sugar
1 pint fresh strawberries,
    washed, then hulled and
    dried

Preheat oven to 350°F.

Press the coconut into the pie pan.

In an electric mixer, combine the cheese, eggs, sugar, lemon juice and lemon zest and beat until smooth. Spoon into prepared shell and bake in preheated oven for 20 minutes. Cool, then chill thoroughly.

Whip the cream with the sugar. To serve, top with the whipped cream and decorate with the strawberries.
SERVES 8.

Coeur à la Crème

This is probably one of the most famous and pleasant of cheese desserts. It is also one of the simplest.

Heart-shaped mold or 2½–3-
  cup mold, lined with wet
  cheesecloth
2 8-ounce packages cream
  cheese, softened
¼ cup heavy cream
⅛ teaspoon salt
2 tablespoons powdered sugar
1 tablespoon apricot brandy
Fresh strawberries or raspberries for garnish

Blend all ingredients except berries until smooth and pour into prepared mold. Chill thoroughly. Invert onto platter, surround with fresh strawberries or raspberries.
SERVES 12.

Cheese Delights

My mother prepared this delicious dessert for us. Even though it is not a cheesecake, it certainly belongs among the great cheese dessert recipes.

2½ cups small curd dry
  cottage cheese
4 eggs
3 tablespoons sugar
2 teaspoons lemon or orange
  zest
½ teaspoon vanilla
Pinch salt
All-purpose flour
Butter

Combine all ingredients except the flour and butter. Spoon onto lightly floured waxed paper, shape into a roll 2″ thick, and wrap tightly in waxed paper. Chill at least an hour.

Cut cheese roll into ½″ slices, dust cut sides with flour, and saute in hot butter until golden brown on both sides. Dust with powdered sugar and serve with sour cream and/or fruit preserves. Delish.
SERVES 4–6.

Macaroon Cheese Whip

Originally this dessert was put in a 2½-quart mold. I have since tried it in individual molds, fluted paper cookie cups, and best of all in a chocolate candy shell or in individual serving chocolate shells. You be the judge.

2 quarts fresh strawberries, washed, hulled and dried

1½ cups sugar

2 cups heavy cream

1½ cups almond macaroons, broken into small pieces

3 8-ounce packages cream cheese

¼ cup milk

½ cup fresh orange juice

3 tablespoons grated orange zest

3 packages unflavored gelatin

½ cup water

Halve 1 quart of strawberries, cover with the sugar, and let stand at room temperature at least 2 hours, shaking occasionally.

Combine the cream with the macaroon pieces and let stand until softened.

Beat the cheese with the milk until smooth, add orange juice and zest, and blend well.

Combine the gelatin with the water and heat, stirring, until completely dissolved.

Drain sugared berries and add their juice to the gelatin, then add gelatin to the cheese mixture, blending thoroughly. Gently fold in the drained strawberries.

Whip the macaroon-cream mixture until thick and fold into the strawberry mixture. Pour into the mold or molds and chill until firm. If in large mold, unmold onto serving platter, and serve garnished with the reserved strawberries.
SERVES 10.

Cakes and Tortes

Basic Dessert Sponge
Golden Sponge Cake
Texas Beer Cake
Texas Bourbon Cake
Instant Genius Angel Food Cake
Conestoga Wagon Spice Cake
Sour Cream Spice Cake
Miss Grimble's Bûche de Noël
My Mother's Honey Cake

§ FRUIT-FLAVORED CAKES §
Orange Date Cake
Calvados Apple Cake
Ambrosial Pineapple Upside-Down Cake
Pineapple Spice Cake
Raspberry Cream Cake
Mrs. Rosen's Strawberry Roll
Texas Fruit Cake

§ CHOCOLATE CAKES §
French Chocolate Cake
Gertie's Chocolate Fudge Cake
Last Minute Chocolate Fudge Cake
My Favorite Chocolate Roll
Chocolate Sheet Cake
Chocolate Coconut Tea Ring
Chocolate Supreme
Cupcakes

(Continued)

§ TORTES §

Hungarian Dobos Torte
Polka Dot Torte
Date Sponge Torte
Hungarian Linzer Torte
Apricot Rum Torte
Chestnut Angel Torte
Chocolate Texas Pecan Torte

Basic Dessert Sponge

Every housewife should learn to make this cake. It freezes beautifully and lends itself to butter cream fillings, fruit fillings, or whipped cream fillings. A trick I learned from my wonderful French bakers is to freeze the cake before attempting to slice it into 3 or 4 layers!

9" cake pan, buttered lightly
8 eggs, separated
2½ cups sugar
½–1 teaspoon pure orange extract, lemon extract, almond extract, vanilla, or Kahlua—or let your imagination be your guide
1½ cups cake flour
2 teaspoons baking powder

Preheat oven to 350°F.

Combine the egg yolks with the sugar and beat until light and lemon-colored. Add the flavoring of your choice. Sift flour and baking powder, and blend into egg mixture. Whip the egg whites until stiff, and gently but thoroughly fold into cake batter. Pour into prepared pan and bake for 30–35 minutes. Cake is done when it springs back when touched. Invert cake to cool as you would any sponge cake by balancing pan on two other cake tins. Cool then freeze before slicing.

When cake is filled and topped it will serve 10–12.

Just remember, the flavoring chosen should match or complement the filling and topping.

Golden Sponge Cake

This lovely creation is particularly welcome in the summer when fresh berries are available.

9" tube pan, completely free
   of grease
2 cups cake flour
1¾ cups sugar
3 teaspoons baking powder
¾ teaspoon salt
½ cup vegetable oil
⅔ cup water
7 room-temperature eggs,
   separated
1 tablespoon lemon juice
2 teaspoons lemon zest
1 teaspoon vanilla
½ teaspoon cream of tartar
Powdered sugar
Berries

Preheat oven to 325°F.

Sift flour before measuring, then resift with sugar, baking powder, and salt into large bowl of electric mixer. Add the oil and the water and blend on low speed for 3 minutes. Beat egg yolks until light and lemony and add to batter. Continue to beat on medium speed for 4 to 7 minutes, then add the flavorings and blend. Beat the egg whites with the cream of tartar until stiff but not dry. Fold the yolk mixture very gently into the beaten egg whites, then spoon into tube pan and bake for about 1 hour. Invert the cake and allow to cool for about 1½ hours. Remove from pan. To serve, dust with powdered sugar. Pass berries.

SERVES 12.

Texas Beer Cake

There's nothing better after a barbecue dinner.

10" tube pan, buttered
2 cups dark brown sugar,
   packed
1 cup vegetable shortening
3 eggs, beaten
3 cups all-purpose flour, sifted
½ teaspoon salt
1 teaspoon baking soda
2 teaspoons baking powder
2 teaspoons ground cloves

Preheat oven to 350°F.

Cream brown sugar with the shortening, add eggs and mix well.

Sift 2½ cups flour with the dry ingredients and spices. Add the flour mixture to the sugar mixture alternately with the beer, beating well after each addition.

Sprinkle the ½ cup reserved flour over the nuts, raisins, and dates and fold into the batter. Spoon into prepared pan and bake for 1 hour,

2 teaspoons allspice
2 teaspoons cinnamon
2 cups beer
1 cup chopped pecans
½ cup raisins
½ cup pitted and chopped
  dates

until sides of cake leave pan. Cool in pan, invert over a serving plate, then remove from pan. SERVES 16.

Texas Bourbon Cake

Before you start I must tell you that Texas is mighty proud of its state tree—the pecan. This is just one of the many creations from the Lone Star State. I know ya'll will cotton to it!

10" tube pan, buttered
4 sticks butter
1 pound brown sugar, sifted
6 eggs
4 cups all-purpose flour, sifted
1 teaspoon baking powder
1 cup bourbon, a good drink-
  ing brand
Scant ½ teaspoon nutmeg
2½ cups seedless raisins
2 cups chopped pecans
Extra all-purpose flour
Confectioners' sugar

Preheat oven to 300°F.

Combine butter and sugar and beat in electric mixer until creamy. Add eggs, one at a time, and blend after each addition.

Resift flour with baking powder and add to batter alternately with the bourbon. Mix well and add nutmeg.

Dust raisins and pecans lightly with extra flour and fold into batter. Spoon into prepared tube pan and bake for 2 hours and 15 minutes. Cool for about 10 minutes, then remove from pan. To decorate, dust with confectioners' sugar. SERVES 12–16.

Instant Genius Angel Food Cake
(A Lavish Dessert for Emergencies)

Ordinarily I do not like to use prepared baking mixes, but if you are willing to experiment and elaborate on them, such mixes can occasionally produce highly satisfying results. The following recipe has saved me socially on many occasions when unexpected guests arrived and I had to whip up a suitably luxurious dessert in an hour or so. In fact, it once saved the day for me professionally. One afternoon the owner of a famous restaurant suddenly informed me that he would arrive in less than two hours to sample our pastries—and in addition to my usual array, he wanted me to present him with something new, luscious, and distinctive for a restaurant he was about to open on New York's fashionable East Side. I immediately thought of a special angel food cake recipe in my files, but we had no time to prepare it from scratch; so I whipped up a reasonable facsimile of this version from a neighborhood supermarket. The restaurateur pronounced it delectable, and my more elaborate version won a permanent place on his menu.

CAKE:
1 package Duncan Hines Angel Food Cake Mix
2–3 tablespoons instant powdered coffee (not freeze-dried)

Follow the instructions on the box of cake mix precisely, with this exception: add 2–3 tablespoons of instant coffee to the flour mixture before blending it in. (If you prefer a stronger flavor you can add up to 4 tablespoons of coffee, but I prefer a more subtle flavor.) Continue to follow the instructions on the box for baking. When the cake is done, remove it from the oven, invert it, and remove pan when cool.

FROSTING:
8 tablespoons butter, at room temperature
2½–3 cups sifted confectioners' sugar
Pinch salt
2–4 tablespoons milk or cream
3–4 tablespoons instant powdered coffee
½ cup sliced, toasted almonds

Cream the butter with the sugar and salt, adding the milk or cream as needed to reach the desired consistency. Add the instant coffee to taste. Beat the mixture until fluffy and spread over the top and sides of the cake, swirling with the back of a spoon. Garnish with the toasted almonds.
SERVES 8–10.

VARIATION:
This recipe can be varied to make a chocolate angel food cake. Simply substitute baking cocoa for the instant powdered coffee and use pecan halves instead of almonds.

Conestoga Wagon Spice Cake

One of the most reliable sources for wonderful cakes was the back of the Imperial Cane Sugar boxes. One in particular, that disappeared from print many years ago, was a favorite in our household. As a matter of fact, after my older daughter married and moved fifty miles away to Corsicana, Texas, her request when we visited was a pair of these cakes.

9" × 9" × 2" pan, lined
   with wax paper
1 stick butter or margarine
2 cups light brown sugar,
   firmly packed
3 eggs, separated
2 cups sifted cake flour
¼ teaspoon salt
1 teaspoon baking soda
2 teaspoons cinnamon
1 teaspoon ground cloves
½ teaspoon nutmeg
1 cup sour cream

Preheat oven to 350°F.
   In an electric mixer, cream the butter and sugar until fluffy. Add the egg yolks and beat again. Sift flour with dry ingredients three times and add alternately with the sour cream to the batter. Beat egg whites until stiff and gently fold into mixture. Pour batter into prepared pan and bake for about 50 minutes. Cool 5–10 minutes before removing pan. Can be served plain, dusted with powdered sugar, or frosted with Old-Fashioned Penuche Icing (p. 183).
SERVES 10–12.

Sour Cream Spice Cake

This pound cake originated in Denmark and is worth every calorie.

9" × 5" × 2¾" loaf pan,
   buttered
1½ cups all-purpose flour
1 teaspoon baking soda
2 tablespoons orange zest
1 tablespoon lemon zest
1½ teaspoons cardamom
½ teaspoon ground allspice
1 stick butter
1 cup sugar
½ teaspoon vanilla
3 eggs
1 cup sour cream

Preheat oven to 350°F.

Combine the flour with the baking soda, zests, and spices. In an electric mixer, beat butter and sugar until light and lemony. Add the vanilla, then beat in the eggs, one at a time. Add dry ingredients alternately with the sour cream. When blended, spoon batter into prepared pan and bake for about 1 hour. Remove loaf from pan and cool.

SERVES 8.

VARIATION:
3 tablespoons chopped
   almonds
2 tablespoons brown sugar
1 teaspoon cinnamon

Combine all ingredients. Sprinkle on top of batter and bake as above.

Miss Grimble's Bûche de Noël

This is the basic recipe we use each year for our annual Christmas display. Each family or province in France has their own garnish for the yule log. We vary depending on which French baker finishes the log.

Use 15" × 10" × 1" cookie
   sheet, lined with heavy
   duty foil, and butter the foil

CAKE:
4 eggs
1 cup sugar
5 tablespoons water
½ teaspoon vanilla
1 cup cake flour, sifted twice

Preheat oven to 375°F.

Beat the eggs until thick; add the sugar and continue to beat until thick. Add water and vanilla and blend well. Sift dry ingredients together and fold into mixture gently but thoroughly. Spread the batter evenly on cookie sheet

1 teaspoon baking powder
¼ teaspoon salt

and bake for 12–15 minutes. Remove from oven and invert onto towel dusted with sugar. Quickly remove the foil, trim the crust, and roll the cake lengthwise in the towel. Chill.

VARIATIONS:
Add 3–4 tablespoons cocoa to the flour mix or the same amount of instant powdered coffee for a mocha flavor.

FILLING:
1 15-ounce can chestnut
    purée, unsweetened
    (Faugier brand)
1 stick butter
4½ ounces bittersweet choco-
    late
3 tablespoons milk
½ cup plus 2 tablespoons
    sugar
1 tablespoon instant powdered
    coffee
1 teaspoon vanilla
1¾ cups heavy cream
6 tablespoons confectioners'
    sugar
1 tablespoon Kahlua
Sweet chocolate shavings for
    garnish
Candied violets for garnish

Combine chestnut purée and butter and blend until smooth. Set aside. Combine chocolate and milk in double boiler over hot water. When melted, add sugar, instant powdered coffee, and vanilla. Pour into the chestnut mix and beat until smooth. Unroll cake and spread the chestnut mixture to the edges. Reroll and chill.

Whip the heavy cream with the confectioners' sugar and Kahlua and spread over cake. Draw the tines of a fork in a zigzag fashion over the log, and place large bittersweet chocolate shavings and candied violets on the log.
SERVES 12.

My Mother's Honey Cake

Than which there is no better!

9" × 13" × 2" pan, lightly
   buttered and floured
4 tablespoons butter
½ cup sugar
¾ cup honey
4 eggs
2 cups cake flour, sifted
1½ teaspoons baking powder
¼ teaspoon baking soda
¼ teaspoon salt
1½ tablespoons instant
   powdered coffee (not
   freeze-dried)
2 tablespoons orange juice
1½ tablespoons orange zest
1 cup walnuts, chopped

Preheat oven to 325°F.

Combine the butter and sugar and beat until light. Add the honey and blend. Beat eggs and add to batter. Combine dry ingredients and sift twice, adding to the batter, blending well. Lastly add the orange juice and zest. Sprinkle walnuts evenly over prepared pan, spoon the batter over all and bake 30–35 minutes. Cut into squares when cool.

SERVES 18.

FRUIT-FLAVORED CAKES

Orange Date Cake

This creation is lovely for any festive occasion.

10" tube pan, buttered and
  floured
2 cups sugar
1 cup vegetable shortening
4 eggs, separated
1 teaspoon baking soda
1 teaspoon baking powder
¼ teaspoon salt
3½ cups all-purpose flour
1½ cups buttermilk
½ cup all-purpose flour to
  sprinkle over fruit and nuts
2½ cups chopped pecans or
  walnuts
2½ cups dates, pitted and
  chopped

GLAZE:
2 cups powdered sugar
3–4 tablespoons grated orange
  zest
1 cup orange juice
1 tablespoon apricot brandy

Preheat oven to 300°F.

In an electric mixer cream the sugar and shortening, then add the egg yolks and blend well. Sift all dry ingredients together and add alternately with buttermilk to batter. Add lightly floured nuts and dates. Beat egg whites until stiff and gently fold into cake mixture. Pour into prepared pan and bake for 1½ hours. Leave in the pan and, while still hot, pierce the cake with an icepick many times and glaze.

Blend all and pour over hot cake. Remove cake from pan when cold.
SERVES 12–14.

Calvados Apple Cake

Easy, quick to prepare, and worth every calorie.

13" × 9" pan, buttered
1 cup raisins
6–8 tablespoons calvados
   brandy
2 cups sugar
½ cup vegetable oil
2 eggs
1 cup chopped walnuts
2 cups all-purpose flour
2 teaspoons cinnamon
2 teaspoons baking soda
¼ teaspoon ground cloves
4 cups Rome apples, peeled,
   cored, and coarsely
   chopped
Lightly sweetened whipped
   cream, for garnish

Put the raisins into the calvados and allow to plump for at least an hour.

Preheat oven to 325°F.

Beat the sugar, oil, and eggs until blended. Beat in the nuts with the raisins and any calvados not absorbed.

Sift the dry ingredients together and add to batter alternately with the chopped apples. Blend well and spoon into prepared pan. Bake in preheated oven for 1 hour, until lightly browned. To serve, top with lightly sweetened whipped cream.

SERVES 8–10.

Ambrosial Pineapple Upside-Down Cake

The title describes this cake perfectly. No more need be said. It was always a favorite for family or friends.

10" cast-iron skillet
4 tablespoons butter
⅔ cup dark brown sugar,
   packed
1 No. 2½ can sliced pine-
   apple, drained
8–10 maraschino cherries
½ cup pecan halves
1 cup cake flour, sifted before
   measuring
1 teaspoon baking powder
⅛ teaspoon salt
4 eggs, separated
1 tablespoon butter, melted

Preheat oven to 325°F.

Melt the butter in the iron skillet, add the brown sugar, and heat until dissolved. Remove from heat and arrange pineapple rounds in the center and half slices around the sides. Fill center of pineapple with maraschino cherries and pecan halves. Set aside. Resift flour with baking powder and salt. In an electric mixer, beat the egg yolks with the melted butter, vanilla, and orange zest. Whip the egg whites until stiff and add the sugar gradually. Combine with the yolk mixture and slowly add the sifted flour. Blend well and spoon over the fruit. Bake in preheated oven for 30 minutes. Let cake stand in pan for five to ten

1 teaspoon vanilla
1 tablespoon orange zest
⅔ cup sugar
1 cup whipped cream, lightly
sweetened, for garnish

minutes, then invert onto cake platter. Serve warm with lightly sweetened whipped cream, flavored with brandy or rum.
SERVES 8.

Pineapple Spice Cake

The blending of creamed cottage cheese in a cake batter insures a moist cake.

13" × 9" loaf pan, buttered
8 tablespoons butter or margarine
12 ounces creamed cottage
cheese
1½ cups dark brown sugar,
firmly packed
2 eggs
2¼ cups all-purpose flour
1 teaspoon baking soda
¼ teaspoon salt
½ cup milk
½ cup drained, crushed pineapple (save balance from
No. 2½ can for topping)
½ teaspoon ground cardamom

Preheat oven to 375°F.

In an electric mixer, cream butter and cheese with the sugar until smooth; add eggs and beat well. Sift flour with baking soda and salt, and add alternately with milk to the batter. Add drained pineapple and cardamom, mix well and pour into buttered pan. Bake at 375°F for 30 minutes. Cool.

ICING:
1 cup dark brown sugar,
firmly packed
5–6 tablespoons butter
¼ cup milk
Balance of the crushed,
drained pineapple
Pinch salt
⅓ cup flaked coconut (op-
tional)

Combine sugar and butter in a saucepan over low heat and stir until melted. Add milk and bring to a rolling boil. Reduce heat and simmer 3–4 minutes. Cool about 15 minutes before adding pineapple and coconut. Spoon over cake.
SERVES 10.

Raspberry Cream Cake

An old time favorite that has never faded in popularity.

2 8" cake pans, buttered
1 stick butter
1 cup sugar
3 eggs, separated
⅔ cup milk
¼ teaspoon salt
25 large honey graham
   crackers, crushed (2 cups)
2½ teaspoons baking powder
1 cup chopped pecans
1 teaspoon vanilla
1 8-ounce jar black raspberry
   jam
2 cups heavy cream, whipped
   with sugar to taste

Preheat oven to 375°F.

In an electric mixer, combine the butter and sugar and blend well. Beat the egg yolks. Add the egg yolks, milk, and salt and beat thoroughly. Combine the crumbs with the baking powder and add to butter mixture. Add ½ cup of chopped pecans and vanilla. Beat egg whites until stiff, and add. Divide the mixture between the two prepared pans and bake in preheated oven 20–25 minutes. Cool. Remove from pan.

Spread raspberry jam on bottom layer, top with whipped cream, then spread top cake layer with raspberry jam and cover top and sides with lightly sweetened whipped cream. Garnish with reserved ½ cup pecans. Refrigerate until time to serve.

SERVES 8–10.

Mrs. Rosen's Strawberry Roll

This lady had few equals in the kitchen. It was always a treat to be served in her home. Better yet, she shared her knowledge with her friends. This is absolutely angelic!

Cookie sheet, covered with heavy, buttered brown paper

CAKE:
4 eggs
1 cup sugar
5 tablespoons water
1 scant cup all-purpose flour
1 teaspoon baking powder
1 teaspoon vanilla
Pinch salt

Preheat oven to 375°F.

Beat eggs well, add sugar, and beat until creamy. Add water and beat about 15 minutes. Combine flour with baking powder and add to batter with vanilla and salt. Beat until smooth. Spread dough on prepared sheet and bake 12–15 minutes. Invert hot cake on tea towel that has been sprinkled with powdered sugar. Cut off hard edges and roll it up while still hot. Chill.

FILLING:
2 cups heavy cream, whipped with sugar to taste
1 pint strawberries, washed, hulled, and sliced
Confectioners' sugar

To fill, unroll the cake gently and spread with whipped cream. Cover with sliced strawberries, reroll and dust with confectioners' sugar.
SERVES 8–10.

Texas Fruit Cake

Texas is famous for pecans and fruit cake. The marriage is perfect, and the cake is very moist.

9" × 13" × 2" baking pan,
   buttered and dusted with
   cocoa
2 cups all-purpose flour
1½ cups sugar
¼ cup cocoa
2 teaspoons baking soda
1 teaspoon cinnamon
½ teaspoon nutmeg
¼ teaspoon allspice
1½ cups applesauce
½ cup milk
1 stick butter, melted
4 tablespoons dark rum
2 tablespoons brandy or
   cognac
1 teaspoon vanilla
1 cup sultana raisins, chopped
1 cup chopped pecans
3 tablespoons orange zest
1 tablespoon lemon zest
⅓ cup extra rum for topping
Confectioners' sugar

Preheat oven to 350°F.

Sift all dry ingredients into large bowl of electric mixer. On low speed, add the applesauce, milk, butter, liquors, and vanilla and blend well. Fold in the raisins and nuts with the orange and lemon zest. Spoon into the prepared pan and bake in preheated oven for about 45 minutes, until cake pulls from the sides of the pan. Remove cake from oven and immediately douse with the additional rum. Let cool in pan for about 15–20 minutes. Remove from pan and age for at least 24 hours. Before serving, dust with powdered sugar.

SERVES 12–14.

CHOCOLATE CAKES

French Chocolate Cake

Don't count the calories, just enjoy!

8" springform, buttered and lined with buttered waxed paper

CAKE:
½ cup sugar
5 eggs, separated
5 ounces sweet chocolate
4 tablespoons water
5 tablespoons all-purpose flour, sifted

FROSTING:
4 egg yolks
¾ cup light corn syrup
6 ounces sweet chocolate
4 tablespoons water
2½ sticks butter
2 tablespoons rum
½ cup chopped almonds or pecans
Powdered sugar

Preheat oven to 350°F.

Combine sugar and egg yolks and beat until lemony and thick. Melt chocolate with water; cool, and add to egg mixture with flour. Beat egg whites to a soft peak and fold gently into batter. Pour the cake mixture into the prepared pan and bake in 350°F oven 45 minutes. Turn out on rack and cool.

Beat yolks until light. Boil syrup to a thread and add to yolks, beating until stiff. Melt chocolate in water and add with creamed butter, when chocolate mix has cooled. Add rum and frost cake. Sprinkle with nuts and powdered sugar.
SERVES 8–10.

Gertie's Chocolate Fudge Cake

Gertie was a superlative cook who worked for the Linzes, a prominent Dallas family, for many years. Her recipes are treasures.

13" × 9" × 2" loaf pan,
    buttered and floured
2 sticks butter
4 squares bitter chocolate
2 cups sugar
4 eggs
2 cups chopped pecans or
    slivered almonds
1 cup all-purpose flour, sifted
½ teaspoon baking powder
1 teaspoon vanilla

Preheat oven to 350°F.

Melt butter with chocolate over hot water. Cream sugar and eggs. Add chopped nuts, flour sifted with baking powder, then melted chocolate and butter, and vanilla. Pour into pan and bake for 15–20 minutes.

Ice, while still warm, with any uncooked chocolate icing.

SERVES 8–10.

Last Minute Chocolate Fudge Cake

Easiest recipe I know. Mix right in the cake pan.

9" square pan
⅓ cup butter, melted and
    cooled
2 ounces premelted, un-
    sweetened chocolate-flavor-
    ed product (2 envelopes)
1 egg
1 cup sugar
1¼ cups instant flour
½ teaspoon baking soda
½ teaspoon salt
½ teaspoon vanilla
¾ cup water
½ cup semisweet chocolate
    pieces
½ cup walnuts or pecan
    halves

Preheat oven to 350°F.

Combine all ingredients except chocolate pieces and nuts. Beat with a fork until smooth and creamy, about 2 minutes. Scrape bottom and sides of pan with rubber spatula after 1 minute of beating. Spread batter evenly in pan; sprinkle with semisweet chocolate pieces and arrange walnut or pecan halves over top. Bake in preheated oven about 30 minutes. Cool in pan and cut in squares.

SERVES 8–10.

My Favorite Chocolate Roll

After serving this, you will be heralded "Queen of the Kitchen!"

Cookie sheet, buttered, covered with a layer of waxed paper, and buttered
5 eggs, separated
¾ cup sugar
6 ounces sweet chocolate
3 tablespoons cold water
1 teaspoon plus ½ teaspoon vanilla
1 cup heavy cream
3 tablespoons sugar
Confectioners' sugar or cocoa

Preheat oven to 350°F.

Beat the yolks and the sugar until lemony. Melt chocolate with water. Cool, and add to the egg mixture with teaspoon vanilla. Blend well. Fold in stiffly beaten egg whites. Pour the mixture onto the cookie sheet evenly and bake for 10 minutes, then reduce heat to 300°F and bake for another 5 minutes or until lightly browned. Remove from oven and cover the top of the cake with a cold wet cloth. Chill for 1 hour. Remove the cloth and loosen the cake from the pan. Turn out on fresh piece of waxed paper. Now remove paper from cake. Whip cream with sugar and ½ teaspoon vanilla. Spread cake with flavored and sweetened whipped cream, and roll up like jelly roll. Dust top with confectioners' sugar or cocoa. Refrigerate until ready to use.
SERVES 8–10.

Chocolate Sheet Cake

A lady by the name of Caroline gave me this little gem!

Cookie sheet, buttered
8 squares bitter chocolate
2 sticks butter
2 cups sugar
4 eggs, beaten
2 teaspoons vanilla
1 cup all-purpose flour, sifted
2½–3 cups chopped pecans or
   walnuts

Preheat oven to 350°F.

   Melt chocolate and butter together in a saucepan. Add the sugar, blend well, then add the beaten eggs and vanilla. Blend the flour and the chopped nutmeats into the mixture and spread on prepared cookie sheet. Bake for 25 minutes.

TOPPING:
1½ cups confectioners' sugar
Light cream

Blend the confectioners' sugar with enough cream to make the right consistency to spread, and top cake. Cut into squares while still warm.
MAKES 30–35 SQUARES.

Chocolate Coconut Tea Ring

Cookie sheet, buttered
2 cups all-purpose flour
3 teaspoons baking powder
½ teaspoon salt
4 tablespoons shortening
¾–1 cup milk
½ of 7-ounce bar semisweet
   chocolate, chopped
1⅓ cups shredded moist
   coconut
2 tablespoons sugar
¼ teaspoon cinnamon
Melted butter or margarine
Confectioners' sugar

Preheat oven to 375°F

   Sift flour, baking powder, and salt together; cut in shortening, and add enough milk to make soft dough. Roll out ½ inch thick on floured board. Shape into oblong 10″ × 6½″ × ¼″. Sprinkle chocolate, coconut, sugar, and cinnamon on dough and roll up jelly roll fashion. Moisten edges and seal. Brush with melted shortening. Place in circle on greased baking sheet and bake 40 minutes. Cover with powdered sugar and serve hot.
SERVES 6–8.

Chocolate Supreme

This cake is a total surprise, both in texture and flavor.

1½ quart buttered glass baking dish
1 cup flour, sifted
Pinch salt
2 teaspoons baking powder
2 tablespoons butter
1¼ cups sugar
½ cup milk
1½ ounces bitter chocolate,
  melted
1 teaspoon vanilla
½ cup brown sugar, packed
4 tablespoons cocoa
1 cup water
1 cup heavy cream
3 tablespoons sugar
1 teaspoon vanilla

Preheat oven to 350°F.

Combine flour, salt, and baking powder, and sift. In an electric mixer cream butter and ¾ cup sugar until lemony. Add sifted ingredients alternately with milk, blending well. Stir in the melted chocolate and vanilla and pour batter into prepared dish. Make a sauce by combining the brown sugar, reserved ½ cup of sugar, cocoa, and water. Gently spoon this sauce over the batter and bake in preheated oven for 45–50 minutes. Unmold cake when cold. Whip cream with sugar and vanilla and serve with cake. Shaved bittersweet chocolate curls are a nice addition.
SERVES 6–8.

Cupcakes

Any chocolate cake batter can be used for cupcakes. Butter tins or put paper cups into tins and fill two thirds full of batter. Bake for 20 minutes in 375°F oven. Cool and ice.
MAKES 18–24 CUPCAKES FROM MOST CAKE BATTERS.

TORTES

Hungarian Dobos Torte

This is the real McCoy! And it *is* worth the effort involved.

FROSTING:

4 *squares bitter chocolate*
2 *sticks sweet butter*
1 *teaspoon vanilla*
1 *cup sugar*
¼ *cup water*
6 *egg yolks*
8–10 *hazelnuts, toasted and chopped*

TORTE:

6 8-*inch cake pans, buttered (loose bottom pans preferred)*
1 *cup sifted flour*
2 *tablespoons cocoa*
6 *eggs, separated*
½ *cup sugar, divided*

Melt the chocolate. Cream the butter and vanilla together until butter is light and fluffy. Set aside.

Combine sugar and water in pan and bring to a boil, stirring gently until sugar is dissolved. Cover saucepan and boil syrup gently for 5 minutes, to melt down any crystals clinging to sides of pan. Uncover and continue cooking to thread stage, 230–234°F on candy thermometer. Remove from heat and set aside.

Beat egg yolks until thick and lemony and gradually pour in the syrup in a thin stream while beating constantly. Beat until consistency of thick butter. Cool completely, then beat this mixture into the butter mixture until just blended. Gradually blend in the chocolate and hazelnuts. Set in refrigerator to chill.

Preheat oven to 350°F.

Sift flour and cocoa and set aside. Cream egg yolks and ¼ cup sugar until lemony. Beat egg whites and gradually add the other ¼ cup sugar. Beat until peaks are formed. Gently spread yolk mixture over beaten whites. Sift the flour mixture gently and gradually over the egg mixture and fold in. Spoon equal amounts of batter into greased pans. Bake in oven for 15 minutes. The batter can be baked in two separate baking periods: three at a time, then repeat. Remove cakes to cooling racks and cool right side up. Remove icing from refrigerator and beat until fluffy. Spread frosting ⅛″ thick, stack another cake on top. Repeat on four of the layers. Cover with the fifth, but do not ice. Frost sides of cake and return to refrigerator. Also return remaining frosting to refrigerator. Place sixth layer on lightly buttered cookie sheet, and lightly butter a small area of baking sheet around layer so caramel icing will not adhere if it runs off. With back of knife blade, make 16–18 equally spaced wedge-shaped indentations on top of cake, but do not cut cake apart.

CARAMEL TOPPING:
¾ cup sugar

Melt in a heavy skillet over low heat, stirring constantly and pressing out lumps. Cook until smooth and golden brown. Remove from heat and quickly pour onto sixth layer. Spread evenly, working quickly before it hardens, and score caramel along indentations in cake. Remove cake and frosting from refrigerator, spread frosting on top of fifth layer and cover with caramel-covered sixth layer. Frost sides of sixth layer and trim edges of cake with any remaining chocolate frosting. Return to refrigerator and chill until icing is firm. Cut cake with knife dipped in hot water.
SERVES 16–18.

Polka Dot Torte

A Viennese favorite that will soon be yours because it is delicious and easy to make.

9" springform
5 eggs, separated
¾ cup sugar
¾ teaspoon grated lemon rind
¾ cup ground almonds
¼ teaspoon salt
1½ tablespoons cornstarch
2½ ounces grated sweet dark chocolate
3½ tablespoons finely rolled bread crumbs
Confectioners' sugar

Preheat oven to 350°F.
Beat the egg yolks with the sugar and lemon rind until light and creamy. Add nuts.
Beat egg whites with salt until stiff; now fold into yolk mixture. Divide the batter in half. Add cornstarch to one half and chocolate and bread crumbs to other half. Drop the batter by alternate spoonfuls into a dry springform and bake in oven for 50–60 minutes. Cool in the pan and release sides. Dust with confectioners' sugar and serve with plain or sweetened whipped cream.
SERVES 10–12.

Date Sponge Torte

There are no superlatives left to describe this cake. It has stood the test of friend and family alike—what more can I say? Try it, I know you will agree. This cake may be served the same day as baked, but I feel it is better served the following day, as the flavor seems to set. Serve this with whipped cream flavored with curaçao or Grand Marnier.

10" tube pan
4 ounces bitter chocolate
1 cup milk
2 cups sugar, divided
4 eggs, separated
1¼ cups cake flour
¼ teaspoon salt
2½ teaspoons baking powder
¾ teaspoon vanilla
1 cup pitted chopped dates
1½ tablespoons grated orange rind
½ cup ground nuts, optional
Confectioners' sugar

Preheat oven to 325°F.

Melt chocolate in top of double boiler. Add milk and 1 cup sugar and cook until smooth. Beat egg yolks until light and lemony with second cup sugar. Sift flour before measuring and resift with salt and baking powder. Add to chocolate mixture with vanilla. Fold in dates, orange rind, and optional nuts, and beat well. Beat egg whites until stiff and gently fold into batter. Pour into dry tube pan and bake in oven for 50–60 minutes. Cool in pan, remove and dust with confectioners' sugar.
SERVES 10–12.

Hungarian Linzer Torte

Another real McCoy!

2 9-inch pans, greased

TORTE:
2¼ cups sifted flour
1 tablespoon cocoa
2 sticks sweet butter
1⅓ cups sugar, divided
8 eggs, separated

Preheat oven to 350°F.

Sift flour with cocoa, and divide into four portions.

Cream butter with ⅔ cup sugar until light and fluffy. Add egg yolks, one at a time, beating well. Beat egg whites until frothy and gradually add the other ⅔ cup sugar. Beat until rounded peaks are formed. Gently spread egg whites over yolk mixture. Sift each portion of flour-cocoa mix over the egg mixture, folding very gently. Fold until just blended. Gently pour batter into pans and bake in oven for 30 minutes. Cool and remove from pans to rack.

FILLING:
⅓ cup thick raspberry preserves

Spread evenly over one layer, top with second layer.

FROSTING:
3 ounces semisweet chocolate
1 stick sweet butter
16 whole, blanched almonds

Melt chocolate in top of double boiler. Remove from heat and add the butter, stirring until completely melted. Cool frosting slightly then spread evenly over top and sides. Before frosting is firm, garnish edge of torte with almonds.
SERVES 10–12.

Apricot Rum Torte

I like this combination, and I think you will too.

*2 9" cake pans, greased and
    floured*

TORTE:
2 eggs
¼ teaspoon salt
1 cup sugar
1 teaspoon rum flavoring
½ cup milk
1 tablespoon butter
1 cup all-purpose flour, sifted
1 teaspoon baking powder

Preheat oven to 350°F.

Beat the eggs until thick and light. Add salt, sugar, and rum flavoring. In a saucepan, bring milk and butter to boiling point and blend gradually into egg mixture.

Combine flour and baking powder, sift, and fold into batter. Blend well, then spoon into prepared pans and bake 35–40 minutes. Cool 5–10 minutes and remove from pans.

SYRUP:
1 cup sugar
1 cup extra-strong coffee
¼ cup rum

Combine sugar and coffee over low heat until sugar dissolves, then boil for 3 minutes. Add the rum. Spoon the syrup slowly over the tops of the still warm cakes until all is absorbed. Chill the cake, then split the layers carefully and fill.

FILLING:
⅓ cup sugar
Pinch salt
¼ cup all-purpose flour
1 cup milk
2 egg yolks, beaten
1 tablespoon rum

Combine sugar, salt, and flour in top of double boiler, add milk, and cook over low heat, stirring, until thickened. Cover and cook about 10 minutes. Add a little of the hot mixture to the egg yolks slowly, then the balance and cook 2–3 minutes longer, stirring constantly. Add the rum and chill.

TOPPING:
1 cup heavy cream
1 tablespoon sugar
⅓ cup thick apricot preserves

Fill the split layers of cake with the chilled rum cream. Whip the cream with the sugar. Garnish the top with thick apricot preserves and top with lightly sweetened whipped cream.
SERVES 8.

Chestnut Angel Torte

I like chestnuts in any form—but particularly in tortes or in creams.

7" springform, buttered and
  floured
8 tablespoons butter
½ cup sugar
2 eggs, separated
½ cup chestnut purée, un-
  sweetened (Faugier brand)
½ cup all-purpose flour
1½ teaspoons baking powder
½ cup thick apricot preserves
1½ tablespoons brandy
4 ounces semisweet chocolate
4 tablespoons butter
Sweetened whipped cream for
  garnish

Preheat oven to 375°F.

Combine butter and sugar in electric mixer. When light and fluffy add the egg yolks and beat well. Add the chestnut purée and blend again. Sift the flour with the baking powder and add to mixture. Beat egg whites until stiff and gently fold into batter. Spoon into prepared springform and bake about 45 minutes.

Remove from oven and cool, then chill and cut torte into two layers.

Combine apricot preserves and brandy in saucepan and bring to a boil, then spread on bottom layer while hot. Put top layer in place.

Melt chocolate with butter over hot water and spread while warm over top and sides of torte, after the torte has cooled. Serve with lightly sweetened whipped cream.
SERVES 6–8.

Chocolate Texas Pecan Torte

Leave it to us to come up with something new, different and delicious!

3 8-inch or 2 10-inch cake pans, lined with buttered wax paper
3 cups pecans
6 eggs, separated
1½ cups sugar
3 tablespoons all-purpose flour
1 teaspoon salt
3 tablespoons Jamaica rum
½ cup heavy cream
2 tablespoons confectioners' sugar
1 cup semisweet chocolate bits
½ cup sour cream

Preheat oven to 350°F.

Put 1 cup of pecans in blender at a time and whirl until very fine. Beat egg yolks until very light, then beat in sugar, flour, salt, 2 tablespoons rum and nuts. Mix well, then fold in egg whites beaten stiffly, but not dry. Pour into pans and bake about 25 minutes. Cool and remove from pans.

A few hours before serving, whip the heavy cream with the confectioners' sugar and 1 tablespoon of rum and spread between cake layers. Melt the chocolate bits, fold in sour cream, and spread over the top of the cake. Refrigerate until served.

SERVES 8–10.

Pies and Tarts

§ SHELLS §

Rich Golden Pastry Shell
Sweet Pastry Dough
Fruit Pastry Shell
Pâte Sucrée
Pâte Brisée
Cream Cheese Pastry Shell
Chocolate Candy Shell
Angel Pie Crust

§ PIES §

Almond Mocha Chiffon Pie
Black Bottom Chiffon Pie with Brandy
Coffee Chiffon Pie
Chocolate Angel Pie
Caramel Chocolate Pie
Satin Pie
Big Mary's Chocolate Pie
Double Chocolate Pie
Banana Chocolate Plantation Pie
Maple Syrup Meringue Pie
Mrs. Limebarger's Rum Cream Pie
Southern Molasses Pie
Texas Pecan Pie
Orange Pecan Pie
Osgood Pie
New Orleans Chocolate Pecan Pie

(Continued)

§ FRUIT PIES §

For Cobbler Lovers
Deep Dish Fruit Pies
Apple Cheddar Pie
Applesauce Pie
Green Tomato Apple Pie
Apple Pear Pie
Apple Raisin Pie
Apricot Pie
Blueberry Pie
Cherry Apple Pie
Garden-Fresh Fig Pie
Whole Lemon Country Pie
Italian Plum Pie
Rhubarb and Fruit Pie
Summer Strawberry Pie
Not Just Another Pumpkin Pie

§ TARTS §

Sugar Cookie Fruit Tart
Tarte Tatin
Apricot Cheese Rum Tart

SHELLS

Rich Golden Pastry Shell

Pastry making has truly become as easy as pie! Tender, rich, and delicious pastry can be made in a matter of minutes and with great imagination!

2½ cups all-purpose flour
1 teaspoon salt
¾ cup lard, shortening, or
  half and half
⅓ cup ice water

Sift flour and salt into mixing bowl. Cut shortening into mixture with pastry blender until mixture looks like coarse meal. Add water, 1 tablespoon at a time. Gather the dough into a ball and divide in half. Wrap in waxed paper and chill for at least an hour.

Roll out each half on a lightly floured board until ⅛″ thick.

YIELD: TWO-CRUST PIE SHELL FOR 9″ PIE.

For a richer crust, increase shortening to 1 cup.
For a one-crust pie shell, use:

1½ cups flour
½ teaspoon salt
½ cup shortening
3 tablespoons ice water

PASTRY SHELL VARIATIONS

Cheese—Blend in ½ cup grated cheddar cheese with the shortening.

Chocolate—To the one-crust pie shell add 4 tablespoons cocoa and 3 tablespoons powdered sugar or 4 tablespoons finely grated semisweet chocolate with powdered sugar.

Lemon—Add 1 tablespoon lemon zest and 1 tablespoon lemon juice plus 1 tablespoon powdered sugar.

Mocha—To the one-crust pie shell add 3 tablespoons cocoa or chocolate with 3 tablespoons powdered sugar and 1 teaspoon instant powdered coffee.

Nut—Add ½ cup ground walnuts or pecans to flour-shortening mixture before adding water.

Orange—Add 2 tablespoons grated orange zest and substitute orange juice for water, plus 1 tablespoon powdered sugar.

Sweet Pastry Dough

This dough will freeze.

2 teaspoons sugar
½ teaspoon salt
12 tablespoons butter, softened
2 eggs
2 tablespoons milk
2½ cups flour

In an electric mixer, combine the sugar, salt, and butter. Blend quickly, then add the eggs and milk and mix well. Now add the flour and blend again. Remove from bowl, wrap in waxed paper and refrigerate.
YIELD: DOUBLE CRUST FOR 10″ PIE.

Fruit Pastry Shell

A good crust for a fruit pie, particularly cherry.

2 cups flour
2 tablespoons confectioners'
  sugar
1¼ teaspoons sugar
¾ teaspoon salt
10–11 tablespoons butter
1 egg yolk, beaten
1½ tablespoons water

Sift all dry ingredients in mixing bowl. Cut butter into flour mixture with pastry blender. Handle the mixture quickly. Add the beaten egg yolk with the water, shape into a ball, wrap in waxed paper and refrigerate for at least ½ hour.
YIELD: BOTTOM AND LATTICE-TOP FOR A 9″ OR 10″ PIE.

Pâte Sucrée

This is a very special pastry crust for tarts or flans.

12 tablespoons butter
⅓ cup sugar
1 egg
2 cups all-purpose flour
½ teaspoon salt

Cream the butter and sugar together and add the egg. Blend well. Sift the flour with the salt and gradually blend into the sugar-butter mixture. This will give you a good cookie dough consistency. If necessary, add a few drops of ice water. Collect the dough and roll into a ball. Cover with plastic wrap or foil and refrigerate until ready to use. Chill.

YIELD: SINGLE CRUST FOR 9″ PIE.

Pâte Brisée

When the French pastry cook wanted a pie shell for dessert, he always used butter.

2 cups sifted flour
1 teaspoon salt
2 sticks cold butter
¼ cup ice water

Combine flour and salt together in chilled bowl. Using a pastry blender or two knives, cut in the cold butter as quickly as possible. When the mixture is pebbly, moisten it little by little with the ice water. When there is just enough to make the dough adhere, shape it into a ball, wrap it in waxed paper, and chill several hours. To use, divide into two parts, one slightly larger than the other, and roll to ⅛″ thickness.

YIELD: DOUBLE CRUST FOR A 9″ PIE.

Cream Cheese Pastry Shell

Even the novice can't fail with this crust. It adapts well for fruit-filled pies.

10" pie plate, unbuttered
1 3-ounce package cream
   cheese
1 stick butter
1 cup all-purpose flour, •
   unsifted
⅛ teaspoon salt
2 teaspoons lemon zest

Cream the cheese and butter together, then add the flour, salt, and lemon zest. When completely blended, work evenly onto bottom and sides of pie plate. Refrigerate until ready to use.
YIELD: SINGLE CRUST FOR 9" OR 10" PIE.

Chocolate Candy Shell

This gorgeous pie "crust" can be filled with 3–3⅓ cups of softened ice cream or other filling.

9" pie plate, lined with alumi-
   num foil
2 tablespoons butter, melted
1 6-ounce package semisweet
   chocolate bits
2 tablespoons powdered sugar

Preheat oven to 250°F.
   Sprinkle the foil with the butter and chocolate and place in oven for about 5 minutes, or until chocolate is soft enough to spread. Remove from oven and dust with 2 tablespoons powdered sugar. Using the back of a teaspoon, blend sugar, chocolate, and butter gently over entire inner surface and halfway up the sides. Refrigerate about 30 minutes or until chocolate is set. Gently lift the foil out of the pie plate without breaking the crust. Peel off the foil and return crust to pie plate. Keep refrigerated until ready to fill.
YIELD: SINGLE CRUST FOR 9" PIE.

Angel Pie Crust

Fill this heavenly shell with chocolate pudding or softened ice cream and chill before serving.

8" pie plate, lightly buttered
2 egg whites
⅛ teaspoon salt
⅛ teaspoon cream of tartar
½ cup granulated sugar
½ cup finely chopped pecans
1 teaspoon grated orange zest
½ teaspoon vanilla

Preheat oven to 300°F.

Beat egg whites with salt and cream of tartar until they begin to hold peaks. Gradually beat in the sugar and continue beating until the meringue is stiff and glossy. Fold in the chopped nuts, orange zest, and vanilla, blending lightly but thoroughly. Spread meringue over the bottom of pie dish; build up sides to ½ inch above the rim of pan. Bake in preheated oven for about 50 minutes. Do not brown too much. Let cool completely.

YIELD: CRUST FOR 8" PIE.

PIES

Almond Mocha Chiffon Pie

Chiffon pies are made with a bit of gelatin in the filling, and this enables them to be made higher and lighter than other pies. This version has a special almond crust.

9" pie plate, buttered

CRUST:
4 tablespoons butter
1½ cups crushed chocolate
    wafers
¼ cup finely chopped al-
    monds, not blanched
2 tablespoons powdered sugar

Preheat oven to 350°F.

Melt butter and combine with wafer crumbs, nuts, and sugar. Blend thoroughly. Pat into pie plate and bake in preheated oven for 10 minutes. Cool.

FILLING:
1 envelope gelatin
¼ cup cold, strong black
    coffee
1 cup granulated sugar
½ teaspoon salt
1½ ounces semisweet choco-
    late pieces
1¼ cups hot strong black
    coffee
3 eggs, separated
1 cup heavy cream
1½ teaspoons vanilla
¼ teaspoon cream of tartar
1 tablespoon powdered sugar
¼ cup slivered toasted
    almonds

Soften the gelatin in the cold coffee.

In a saucepan, combine ½ cup of the granulated sugar, salt, and chocolate in the hot coffee and cook over low heat until chocolate is melted.

Beat the egg yolks until thick and lemon colored. Beat in a few spoonfuls of the hot coffee mixture, then slowly pour into the remaining hot mixture, beating as you do so. Cook over low heat, stirring constantly, until thickened. Remove from heat. Add gelatin and stir until dissolved. Cool until almost set; whip until smooth with rotary beater. Mixture should be very light and foamy.

Whip ½ cup of the heavy cream until stiff and add 1 teaspoon of the vanilla. Fold into the chocolate mixture.

Whip the egg whites with the cream of tartar until they hold soft peaks; gradually beat in the remaining ½ cup granulated sugar. Continue beating until thick and glossy. Fold into the chocolate mixture also. Pour into chilled shell and refrigerate several hours.

One hour before serving, whip remaining ½

cup cream and sweeten with powdered sugar. Add remaining ½ teaspoon vanilla. Spread over top of pie. Sprinkle with toasted almonds. Keep chilled until needed.
SERVES 7–8.

Black Bottom Chiffon Pie with Brandy

The snapper in this pie is the gingersnap crust.

10" pie plate, buttered

CRUST:
2 cups gingersnap crumbs
4 tablespoons butter, melted
¼ cup powdered sugar

Blend crumbs with the butter and sugar and press firmly into pie plate.

FILLING:
4 eggs, separated
½ cup dark brown sugar, sifted
¼ teaspoon salt
1¼ tablespoons cornstarch
1½ cups milk, scalded
6 tablespoons brandy
2 squares bitter chocolate, melted
1 teaspoon vanilla
1 envelope gelatin
2 tablespoons cold water
¼ teaspoon cream of tartar
½ cup granulated sugar
Sweetened whipped cream for garnish
Sweet chocolate curls for garnish

In top of double boiler over hot water beat yolks until light. Add the brown sugar that has been sifted with salt and cornstarch. Gradually stir in the scalded milk and 5 tablespoons brandy. Cook over hot water, stirring constantly, until thickened. Remove from heat and set aside.

Measure 1½ cups of the custard into a bowl and stir in the melted chocolate and vanilla. Cool and spoon into prepared pie shell.

Soften gelatin in water and add to balance of custard with 1 tablespoon brandy. Mix well. Cool, but do not let this set.

Beat egg whites with cream of tartar until stiff, then beat in the granulated sugar. Fold egg whites into cooled custard and spoon over the chocolate custard. Chill for at least 3–4 hours.

Before serving, top with the lightly sweetened whipped cream, and garnish with sweet chocolate curls.
SERVES 8–10.

Coffee Chiffon Pie

Laced with Kahlua, this is superb!

CRUST:
Use a 9" Classic Crumb Crust (see p. 3), chilled

Prepare Classic Crumb Crust using chocolate wafers.

FILLING:
1 envelope gelatin
¼ cup cold water
2 tablespoons instant powdered coffee
¾ cup hot water
¼ teaspoon salt
½ cup plus 1 tablespoon sugar
3 eggs, separated
1 tablespoon plus 1 teaspoon Kahlua
1 cup heavy cream
Grated bitter chocolate for garnish

Dissolve gelatin in cold water.

Combine coffee and hot water in top of double boiler. Add salt and ¼ cup of the sugar. Cook over direct heat until dissolved. Remove from heat. Beat egg yolks lightly and slowly add to the hot liquid, stirring constantly. Return to double boiler and cook over simmering water, stirring, until mixture is slightly thickened. Remove from heat and add dissolved gelatin, blending. Add tablespoon of Kahlua and chill until slightly thickened.

Beat egg whites until stiff, gradually adding another ¼ cup sugar. Fold into chilled mixture and turn into prepared shell. Chill until firm, about 2–3 hours.

Whip the cream with the teaspoon of Kahlua and 1 tablespoon sugar. Garnish with the whipped cream and dust with grated bitter chocolate.

SERVES 8.

Chocolate Angel Pie

Desserts are my business, and I find this possibly the most irresistible one in all dessertdom. Dieters fall off their diets and strong men go weak at the sight of it. It is beautiful to behold and luscious to eat.

9" pie plate, buttered lightly

CRUST:
4 egg whites (save yolks for filling)
¼ teaspoon cream of tartar—be sure it is fresh
1 cup granulated sugar

Preheat the oven to 275°F.

Whip the egg whites until foamy. Add the cream of tartar and continue beating. Add the sugar gradually, beating all the while, and continue beating until the egg whites are stiff. Spread the mixture evenly and as smoothly as possible on the bottom and sides of the pie plate, building up the sides carefully so the shell will hold the filling. Bake the meringue at 275°F for one hour. Remove from oven and cool. The crust should be lightly browned. When cool, it will crack slightly like a macaroon.

FILLING:
12 ounces semisweet chocolate
¼ cup hot water
1½ tablespoons instant powdered coffee
1 cup heavy cream
2 tablespoons Kahlua

Melt the chocolate in hot water in the top of a double boiler. Add coffee to chocolate mixture, blend well, and cool. Whip the cream with the Kahlua and fold into mixture. Spoon into meringue shell. Refrigerate for 4–5 hours.

TOPPING:
1 cup heavy cream
4 tablespoons sugar
1 teaspoon vanilla
1 pint fresh strawberries, washed and drained, then hulled and dried. (Do this just before you are ready to use them so they do not become water-logged.)
1 10-ounce bar bitter or semisweet chocolate for shaving

Beat the cream with the sugar and vanilla until it is stiff. Spread it over the top of the filling, swirling it attractively with a spatula. Just before serving, garnish with the strawberries, and grate curls of chocolate over all.
SERVES 8.

Caramel Chocolate Pie

This combination reminds me of chewy caramels covered with chocolate!

CRUST:
Use a 9" prebaked pastry shell

FILLING:
⅔ cup dark brown sugar, packed
⅓ cup all-purpose flour
½ teaspoon salt
2½ cups milk
½ cup Hershey's chocolate syrup
2 egg yolks, well beaten
2 tablespoons butter
¾ teaspoon vanilla
Sweetened whipped cream for garnish
Toasted almonds for garnish

Mix together the brown sugar, flour, and salt until blended. Put into a medium saucepan and add the milk, chocolate syrup, and egg yolks. Cook over medium heat, stirring constantly, until thickened.

Remove from heat and add butter and vanilla. Cool slightly, then pour into prebaked shell and chill for at least 4 hours.

Garnish with lightly sweetened whipped cream and toasted almonds.

SERVES 8.

Satin Pie

And so it is!

CRUST:
Use a 9" prebaked pastry shell

FILLING:
*1 12-ounce package semisweet
   chocolate bits
¼ cup milk
¼ cup granulated sugar
Pinch salt
4 eggs, separated
1 teaspoon vanilla
Sweetened whipped cream*

Combine chocolate, milk, sugar, and salt in top of double boiler and cook over hot water, stirring, until mixture is blended and smooth. Cool slightly. Add yolks, one at a time, beating well after each addition. Blend in the vanilla. Cool to room temperature.

Beat egg whites until stiff and gently fold into the chocolate mixture. Pour into prebaked pie shell and allow to chill for 2–3 hours. Serve with sweetened whipped heavy cream.
SERVES 7–8.

Big Mary's Chocolate Pie

For nearly fifteen years Mary was factotum-extraordinary of our household in Dallas. This is her special chocolate pie made with corn syrup and sour cream.

CRUST:
Use a 9" prebaked pastry shell

FILLING:
*4 ounces sweet chocolate
2 eggs, separated
¼ cup light corn syrup
1 cup sour cream
¼ teaspoon salt
1 cup heavy cream
1 tablespoon powdered sugar
Grated bitter chocolate for
   garnish*

Melt chocolate in top of double boiler over hot water; set aside. Beat egg yolks until thick and lemon colored. Add to the cooled chocolate and blend. Add corn syrup, sour cream, and salt, and blend thoroughly. Beat egg whites until stiff and fold into the mixture. Pour into prebaked shell and chill several hours.

Whip the cream with the sugar. Spread surface of pie with the whipped cream. Chill for an hour. Sprinkle top with grated bitter chocolate if desired.
SERVES 8.

Double Chocolate Pie

This pie has a chocolate-pecan filling with a kind of baked-on chocolate frosting. Be prepared for second helpings!

CRUST:
Use a 9" unbaked pastry shell

FILLING:
2½ ounces bitter chocolate
½ tablespoon butter
¾ cup all-purpose flour, sifted
1 tablespoon baking powder
  plus ½ teaspoon
¼ teaspoon salt
9 tablespoons sugar
½ cup chopped pecans
6 tablespoons milk
1 teaspoon vanilla

Preheat oven to 375°F.

Melt chocolate with butter in the top of a double boiler over hot water; cool. Combine flour, baking powder, salt, and sugar. Sift together. Add pecans. Slowly add milk and vanilla; blend. Add chocolate mixture and stir until smooth. Pour into unbaked shell.

TOPPING:
1½ ounces bitter chocolate
1 cup water
⅔ cup sugar

Combine 1½ ounces chocolate with water and sugar in saucepan and cook over low heat, stirring constantly, until melted. Allow mixture to come to a full boil without stirring. Cook 1 minute. Remove from heat. Gently spoon this mixture over the chocolate filling. Bake in preheated oven until done, about 20 minutes. Serve warm or cold with lightly sweetened, rum-flavored whipped cream or vanilla ice cream.
SERVES 8.

Banana Chocolate Plantation Pie

The original recipe did not call for a layer of bananas on the bottom of the shell. A friend of mine in Dallas suggested the addition as she loves bananas and chocolate. It is a welcome variation.

CRUST:
Use a 9" prebaked pastry shell

FILLING:
1½ cups milk
1 cup granulated sugar
¼ teaspoon salt
3 tablespoons all-purpose flour
2 eggs
1 teaspoon vanilla
3 squares bitter chocolate
1 tablespoon butter
½ cup heavy cream, whipped
1 banana, sliced thinly

Put 1 cup of the milk in the top of a double boiler and scald. Mix all the dry ingredients with remaining ½ cup milk and blend well. Pour into the hot milk mixture and cook, stirring, until thickened. Beat the eggs and add to the hot mixture slowly and cook for another 5 minutes. Remove from heat; add vanilla and cool.

Melt chocolate with butter and add to custard. Chill, then fold in the whipped cream.

Spread sliced banana over bottom of pie shell and pour chocolate mixture on top. Chill 2–3 hours.

This may be garnished with additional whipped cream and sprinkled with shaved bittersweet chocolate.

SERVES 7–8.

Maple Syrup Meringue Pie

CRUST:

9" pie shell made with 2 tablespoons honey graham
crackers and ground
pecans (see Classic Crumb
Crust, p. 3)

FILLING:

1 envelope gelatin
¼ cup cold water
2 eggs, separated
⅔ cup maple syrup
Pinch salt
1 cup milk
½ cup heavy cream
1 teaspoon vanilla

Soften the gelatin in water.

Beat the egg yolks and combine with ½ cup of the syrup and the salt in the top of a double boiler. Gradually add the milk, blend well, and place over hot water. Cook, stirring constantly, until mixture coats a spoon. Remove from heat and blend in gelatin. Chill until thick.

Add balance of syrup to maple mixture and whip.

Beat egg whites to a stiff peak and fold into chilled mixture. Whip the cream with the vanilla. Fold the whipped cream into mixture and spoon into prepared shell. Chill at least 4 hours before serving.

SERVES 8.

Mrs. Limebarger's Rum Cream Pie

Mrs. Limebarger was a neighbor of Mother Hirsch's for over twenty years. This was her favorite pie which she so generously made for the Hirsch family and for which she later divulged the recipe.

CRUST:
Use a 10" prebaked chocolate
pie shell

FILLING:
6 egg yolks, room temperature
1 cup sugar
1 tablespoon gelatin
½ cup water
½ cup dark rum
2 cups heavy cream, whipped
Grated bittersweet chocolate
for garnish

Beat the egg yolks until light and lemony, then add the sugar and continue to beat until blended. In a saucepan, dissolve the gelatin in the water and bring to a boil. Reduce heat and stir until gelatin is dissolved completely. Remove from heat and slowly add the beaten yolks in a steady stream, beating constantly. Cool the mixture, then add the rum and fold in the whipped cream. Pour into prepared shell and chill several hours. To serve, garnish with grated bittersweet chocolate.
SERVES 8–10.

Southern Molasses Pie

This is indigenous to below the Mason-Dixon Line. Try it—you'll like it.

CRUST:
Use a 10" unbaked pie shell

FILLING:
5 eggs, separated
2 cups sugar
1 tablespoon flour
1 cup dark molasses
1 cup heavy cream
1 tablespoon butter, softened
½ teaspoon cinnamon
½ teaspoon cloves
½ teaspoon nutmeg
Pinch salt

Preheat oven to 375°F.

Beat yolks and add 1½ cups of the sugar. Add flour gradually and beat until creamy. Add molasses, cream, butter, spices, and salt. Blend well and pour into prepared shell. Bake 30–40 minutes until firm.

Beat the egg whites until stiff with the remaining ½ cup sugar and pinch of salt. Cover top of pie with meringue, reduce heat to 300°F and bake until golden (about 15 minutes).
SERVES 8–10.

Texas Pecan Pie

Texans have good reason to brag about their pecan pies! Not only is the pecan tree the state tree of Texas, but Texas is one of the nation's largest suppliers of pecans.

CRUST:

Make your favorite 9″ pie shell adding a pinch more salt to the dough, which complements the pecans. Prebake the pie shell at 450° for about 5 minutes.

FILLING:
1 cup pecan halves
3 eggs, beaten
¼ teaspoon salt
¾ cup sugar
1 cup dark Karo syrup
1 stick butter, melted
½ teaspoon vanilla

Preheat oven to 400°F.

Sprinkle pecan halves over prepared shell. Beat eggs with salt until thick and creamy. Gradually add the sugar and beat until well blended. Add syrup, melted butter, and vanilla. Pour mixture over pecans. The pecans will rise to the top and when baked will be beautifully glazed. Bake at 400°F for 10 minutes, reduce heat to 325°F, and continue to bake 30 minutes longer. Serve at room temperature. This lily can be gilded by passing a bowl of lightly sweetened whipped cream or vanilla ice cream when serving.
SERVES 8.

Orange Pecan Pie

This is an unusual twist to pecan pie. It certainly is easy and worth the effort.

CRUST:
Use a 9" unbaked pie shell

FILLING:
1 cup whole pecans
3 eggs
¾ cup sugar
1 cup white Karo syrup
2 tablespoons butter, melted
1 tablespoon orange juice
2 tablespoons grated orange zest

Preheat oven to 350°F.
    Spread pecans in bottom of pie shell. In electric mixer, beat eggs with sugar, add Karo syrup, and melted butter. Blend. Add the juice and zest and pour over the pecans. Bake for 45 minutes until pecans are nicely browned and glazed. Cool to room temperature.
SERVES 8.

Osgood Pie

No one seems to know the origin of this pie or why it is so named. It is popular in Texas.

CRUST:
Use a 9" unbaked pastry shell

FILLING:
3 eggs
1 cup sugar
1 teaspoon cinnamon
½ teaspoon ground cloves
1½ teaspoons cider vinegar
1 teaspoon vanilla
1 cup chopped raisins
1 cup chopped pecans
Sweetened whipped cream

Preheat oven to 350°F.
    Beat the eggs. Gradually add the sugar and beat well. Add the balance of the ingredients except the whipped cream, mix thoroughly and spoon into prepared pastry shell. Bake in preheated oven for 45 minutes. When cool, serve with slightly sweetened whipped cream.
SERVES 8.

New Orleans Chocolate Pecan Pie

Because I am the booziest baker in Manhattan, I have a liquor license. That entitles me to buy booze at wholesale, but more important I receive advance notices of all new liquors offered for sale. Praline is new and the folder suggesting its varied uses accompanied the sample. It is great—do buy it and try it as I did. This is one of the best in the booklet.

CRUST:
Use a 9" unbaked pastry shell

FILLING:
2 eggs
1 cup sugar
4 tablespoons cornstarch
8 tablespoons butter, melted
¼ cup Praline liqueur
1 cup pecans, chopped
*6-ounce package semisweet
    chocolate chips*
*Whipped cream or vanilla ice
    cream for garnish*
Praline liqueur for garnish

Preheat oven to 350°F.
    Beat eggs slightly. Combine sugar and cornstarch and gradually add to eggs, mixing well. Stir in the melted butter. Add the Praline liqueur. Add pecans and chocolate chips. Pour into unbaked pastry shell. Bake 45–50 minutes. Cool. Garnish with whipped cream or a scoop of vanilla ice cream. Spoon 1 tablespoon Praline liqueur over all.
SERVES 7–8.

FRUIT PIES

For Cobbler Lovers

Any fruit pie filling can be turned into a cobbler filling by increasing all ingredients by one half. In this case, only a one-crust dough is necessary for the top.

Use an 8″ round casserole dish. Fill it with fruit and top with the dough, sealing the edges. Brush with melted butter and dust with granulated sugar. Make several slits in the dough to allow steam to escape.

Bake at 425°F for 30 minutes. Serve warm and top with ice cream. SERVES 6–8.

Deep Dish Fruit Pies

As this recipe uses frozen fruits, it is available the year round.

1-quart casserole, buttered

CRUST:
1 recipe Rich Golden Pastry
  Shell (p. 55)

FILLING:
4 cups unsweetened frozen
  berries or fruit, thawed
2 cups sugar
4 tablespoons flour
Juice of one lemon
4 tablespoons port
Light cream
Sweetened whipped cream

Preheat oven to 450°F.

Place fruit or berries in casserole. Blend sugar and flour and mix thoroughly with the fruit. Sprinkle with the lemon juice and port, and cover with the pastry crust. Cut several slits in the crust, brush with cream, and bake for 8 minutes at 450°F. Reduce heat to 350°F and continue to bake a half hour longer, until crust is nicely browned. Serve warm and pass a bowl of lightly sweetened whipped cream. SERVES 4–5.

Apple Cheddar Pie

This is great served with a dollop of sour cream.

CRUST:
Use a 9″ pie shell

Prepare shell (p. 55) substituting sour cream for the ice water, then proceed as usual.

FILLING:
6 tart apples, peeled, cored, and thinly sliced
1 cup sugar
2 tablespoons all-purpose flour
2 teaspoons lemon zest
1 teaspoon orange zest
1 teaspoon cinnamon
⅛ teaspoon ground cloves
⅛ teaspoon salt

Preheat oven to 400°F.
Combine the sliced apples with the sugar, flour, zests, cinnamon, cloves, and salt and spread evenly in prepared pie shell.

TOPPING:
½ cup all-purpose flour
½ cup grated cheddar cheese
¼ cup sugar
⅛ teaspoon salt
¼ cup butter, melted

Blend topping ingredients to a pebble-like consistency and sprinkle over apples. Bake for about 40 minutes, until lightly browned. Cool.
SERVES 8.

Applesauce Pie

This is a first-class, hurry-up dessert that can be made even when there's no fresh fruit available.

9″ pie plate
2 cups honey graham cracker crumbs
1 stick butter, softened
3¼ cups applesauce, home-made if possible
¼ teaspoon cinnamon
¼ teaspoon vanilla
1 cup heavy cream
1 tablespoon sugar

Preheat oven to 400°F.
Combine crumbs and butter. Reserving ⅓ for topping, press onto bottom and sides of pan. Blend applesauce with cinnamon and vanilla and spoon into shell. Dust top with remaining crumbs and bake for 20 minutes. Cool. Whip the cream with the sugar and spread over pie.
SERVES 8.

Green Tomato Apple Pie

An unusual combination, laced with brandy.

CRUST:
*Use a 9″ unbaked double-
    crust pie shell*

FILLING:
½ stick butter
*½ cup dark brown sugar,
    packed*
1 tablespoon lemon zest
⅛ teaspoon cinnamon
⅛ teaspoon nutmeg
*3 large green tomatoes, peeled
    and thinly sliced*
*3 large tart apples, peeled,
    cored, and thinly sliced*
2 tablespoons calvados brandy
Granulated sugar

Preheat oven to 450°F.

Cream the butter with the brown sugar, lemon zest, and spices.

In the pie shell, arrange a layer of tomatoes and apples, sprinkle with sugar mixture. Continue alternating tomatoes and apples with sugar mixture until all are used. Sprinkle with brandy and cover with top crust. Dust top with granulated sugar, make several slashes in crust, and bake in preheated oven for 10 minutes, then reduce temperature to 350°F and continue to bake an additional 35 minutes.

SERVES 6–8.

Apple Pear Pie

An immediate success, especially when Bosc pears are in season.

CRUST:
*Use a 9" unbaked double-
crust pie shell*

FILLING:
*3 cups apples, peeled, cored,
and sliced*
*3 cups pears, peeled, cored,
and sliced*
⅓ cup granulated sugar
⅓ cup dark brown sugar
2 tablespoons all-purpose flour
⅛ teaspoon salt
½ teaspoon lemon zest
1 tablespoon fresh lemon juice
1 tablespoon orange zest
1 tablespoon brandy
½ teaspoon cinnamon
½ cup raisins
2 tablespoons butter
Granulated sugar

Preheat over to 425° F.

Combine the fruits and place half in unbaked pie shell. Combine all remaining ingredients, except butter and extra sugar, and sprinkle half the mixture over the fruit. Add the balance of the fruit, then the remaining mixture. Dot the top with butter and cover with top crust. Make several slashes in crust, sprinkle with extra sugar, and bake 45–50 minutes.
SERVES 8.

Apple Raisin Pie

Apples and raisins marry well, especially when the raisins have been soaked in bourbon, calvados, apple juice, or orange juice until plump.

CRUST:
9" unbaked double-crust pie shell

FILLING:
6 cups apples—Rome, Granny Smith, or Greenings—peeled, cored, sliced
½ cup raisins soaked in 2–3 tablespoons liquor or fruit juice
½ cup toasted chopped pecans
¾–1 cup sugar, depending on apple tartness
2 tablespoons all-purpose flour
1 teaspoon cinnamon
⅛ teaspoon nutmeg
¼ teaspoon salt
¼ stick butter

Glaze the pie shell with thick apricot jam.

Preheat oven to 425°F.

Combine all ingredients except butter in bowl, including liquid. Pour into shell, dot lightly with butter, top with crust. Make several slits in top crust and bake in preheated oven for 50–60 minutes.

SERVES 8.

Apricot Pie

A delicious finale to a winter meal when fresh fruit is unavailable.

CRUST:
Use a 9″ unbaked double-crust pie shell

FILLING:
5 cups canned, drained apricot halves
¾ cup sugar
¼ cup brown sugar
2 tablespoons tapioca
⅛ teaspoon salt
⅛ teaspoon cinnamon
1–2 tablespoons fresh lemon juice

Preheat oven to 400°F.
   Spread fruit in bottom of shell. Blend dry ingredients and sprinkle over fruit, add lemon juice. Cover top with a lattice made of strips of dough. Bake at 400°F for 45 minutes.
SERVES 8.

Blueberry Pie

I am a blueberry freak! Muffins, cake, cobblers, and pie, and best of all, unadorned, in a bowl. The following is my favorite filling.

CRUST:
Use an 8″ unbaked double-crust pastry shell

Line pie shell with dough, leaving a half-inch flap of dough for folding onto top crust.

FILLING:
3 cups fresh blueberries, or 2 cans, drained, or 2 boxes frozen that have been defrosted
½ cup sugar
2 tablespoons all-purpose flour
2 tablespoons fresh lemon juice
1 tablespoon butter, melted
¼ teaspoon salt
Good dash of cinnamon

Preheat oven to 450°F.
   Combine all ingredients and fill pastry shell. Moisten edge of shell, cover with top pastry, and seal the edges. The pastry should be only ⅛″ thick. Make several slits in top crust and bake in preheated oven for 20 minutes; then decrease oven to 350° and continue to bake another 25 minutes.
SERVES 6–8.

Cherry Apple Pie

The "snapper" to this pie is the addition of the preserves.

CRUST:
Use a 9" unbaked double-
   crust pastry shell

FILLING:
4 cups peeled, cored, and
   sliced Granny Smith or
   Greening apples
½ cup sugar
1 tablespoon orange juice
1 tablespoon all-purpose flour
¼ teaspoon salt
6 tablespoons cherry preserves
Sugar

Preheat oven to 300°F.

Combine all ingredients except the preserves and sugar. Toss well to blend, then turn into prepared pie shell. Dot the top with the preserves, cover with the remaining pastry shell. Seal the edges, slash the top several times, dust with sugar, and bake in preheated oven for 30–40 minutes.

SERVES 6–8.

Garden-Fresh Fig Pie

As fig trees were in abundance in our backyard, we enjoyed them in many forms—fresh, preserved, and in this unusual pie.

CRUST:
Use a 9" unbaked pie shell
   with lattice top

FILLING:
3½ cups fresh figs, peeled and
   sliced
3 tablespoons fresh lemon
   juice
1 tablespoon orange juice
1 tablespoon plus 1 teaspoon
   orange zest
3 tablespoons butter
1 cup heavy cream
2 tablespoons sugar

Preheat oven to 450°F.

Mix fresh sliced figs with juices and table-spoon zest and spoon into unbaked shell. Dot with butter and cover with lattice crust. Bake for 10 minutes, then reduce heat to 350°F and continue baking for 25 minutes. Whip the cream with the sugar and teaspoon of orange zest and use to garnish pie.

SERVES 8.

Whole Lemon Country Pie

This pie is a favorite of mine that my bakery introduced to the public without the success I'd anticipated. Probably too tart for New York tastes.

CRUST:
*Use a 9″ unbaked double-
   crust pie shell*

FILLING:
*2 large lemons, sliced paper
   thin (do not peel them)*
2¼ cups sugar
2 tablespoons butter, melted
4 eggs, beaten
Pinch salt
Dash nutmeg
Granulated sugar

Preheat oven to 400°F.

Marinate sliced lemons in sugar for at least 2–3 hours. Add butter, eggs, salt, and nutmeg, mixing to blend, and pour into prepared shell.

Cover the pie with the top crust, dust with sugar, make several slashes in the crust and bake in preheated oven for 10 minutes, then reduce heat to 350°F and continue to bake for 30 minutes. Cool to room temperature.
SERVES 6–8.

Italian Plum Pie

A welcome addition to your summer fruit repertoire.

CRUST:
*Use a 9″ unbaked double-
   crust pastry shell*

FILLING:
*3½ cups fresh Italian prune
   plums, quartered and
   pitted*
⅓ cup water
¾ cup sugar
2 tablespoons cornstarch
Pinch salt
½ cup finely chopped pecans
2 tablespoons butter

Preheat oven to 400°F.

In a medium saucepan, combine plums with water and bring to a boil. Reduce heat and cook for 5–7 minutes.

Combine sugar, cornstarch, and salt and stir into the plum mixture. Continue to cook slowly until thick and transparent, stirring constantly. Remove from heat, add pecans and butter and cool.

Spread marmalade evenly over crust and fill

⅓ cup orange marmalade
Granulated sugar

with plum mixture. Cover with top crust, slash top in several places, dust with granulated sugar, and bake for 45 minutes.

Serve with lightly sweetened whipped cream.
SERVES 8.

Rhubarb and Fruit Pie

A sure sign that spring is on the way. If you have spring fever, this should cure it.

CRUST:
Use a 9" unbaked double-crust pie shell

FILLING:
*2 cups rhubarb, cut into ½"
    pieces
1 cup fresh, cubed pineapple
2 cups fresh strawberries,
    washed, hulled, and sliced
    only if large
1½ cups sugar
6 tablespoons all-purpose
    flour
1 tablespoon orange zest
1 teaspoon lemon zest
⅛ teaspoon salt
2 tablespoons butter, melted
Sugar*

Preheat oven to 450°F.

Combine the fruits with all the ingredients except sugar, toss lightly to coat, and turn into prepared pie shell. Cover with top crust, seal the edges, slash the top, and dust with sugar. Bake in preheated oven for 10 minutes, then reduce oven to 350°F and continue to bake for about 40 minutes, until crust is golden.
SERVES 8.

Summer Strawberry Pie

CRUST:
Use a 10" baked pie shell

FILLING:
5 cups strawberries, washed,
  hulled, and dried
1½ tablespoons cornstarch
2 teaspoons lemon juice or
  orange juice
1¼ cups sugar
Sweetened whipped cream

Be sure to try this with the Cream Cheese Pastry Shell, prebaked (p. 58).

Arrange half of the strawberries in the prebaked pie shell. Mix the cornstarch into the juice. Crush the other half of the berries and place in saucepan with the sugar and cornstarch and fruit juice. Bring to a boil, then reduce heat and cook for about 10–12 minutes, stirring constantly, until sauce is clear. Let cool to room temperature, then spoon over berries in shell. Chill in refrigerator at least an hour before serving. Top with lightly sweetened whipped cream.
SERVES 8–10.

Not Just Another Pumpkin Pie

This is the only pumpkin pie that I have ever enjoyed because it is not thick and heavy. On the contrary, it is light and airy!

CRUST:
Use a 9" unbaked pie shell

FILLING:
2 tablespoons butter, softened
¾ cup sugar
3 eggs
½ teaspoon salt
¼ teaspoon ginger
¼ teaspoon nutmeg
½ teaspoon cinnamon
1 cup canned pumpkin (un-
  seasoned)
1 cup evaporated milk

Preheat oven to 450°F.
In an electric mixer, combine all ingredients. Beat well. Pour into unbaked pie shell and bake 10 minutes at 450°F, then reduce heat to 325°F and continue baking for 45 minutes.
Delicious when served with a thin slice of sharp cheddar cheese, sprinkled with a dash of cinnamon.
SERVES 8.

TARTS

Sugar Cookie Fruit Tart

When fresh fruits are out of season, this is a welcome substitute.

10" pie plate, buttered and
  chilled

CRUST:
5½ tablespoons sugar
10–11 tablespoons sweet
  butter, softened
1 egg
⅛ teaspoon salt
¼ teaspoon vanilla
1⅔ cups cake flour, sifted

Preheat oven to 425°F.

Blend sugar and butter in an electric mixer only until lemony in color. Do not over beat. Lightly mix in the egg, salt, and vanilla, just to blend. Add the flour slowly until the dough is pale yellow and forms a soft mass. Form dough into a ball and wrap in plastic wrap and chill about 2–3 hours.

When ready to use, roll on lightly floured board to about ¼" thick and gently fit the circle of dough onto the pie plate. Save the extra dough for the lattice strip topping. Prebake the shell for 5 minutes at 425°F.

FILLING:
1 8-ounce jar fruit preserve

Spread crust evenly with selected fruit preserve and strip the top in a criss-cross fashion with the leftover cookie dough. Return to oven and bake at 350°F for 25–30 minutes, until crust is a golden brown. Serve at room temperature.
SERVES 8–10.

Tarte Tatin

One of my French bakers taught me how to prepare this lovely upside-down apple tart.

9" pie plate at least 2" deep,
  bottom and sides heavily
  buttered

CRUST:
Use a 9" sweet pastry shell

FILLING:
Sugar
3 cups peeled, cored, and
  sliced tart apples
½ cup sugar
6 tablespoons butter
Whipped cream for garnish

Preheat oven to 375°F.

Cover the bottom of the pie plate with ¼" of sugar. Arrange the sliced apples in neat layers to the top of the pie plate, sprinkle with the sugar, and dot with the butter. Cover the dish with the pastry shell cut to fit. Bake in preheated oven for about 30 minutes. Tart is ready when apples are golden and the sugar is beginning to caramelize. (Bubbles form but do not burst.) Cool for about 5 minutes, then loosen the crust all around. Put a serving platter upside down over the pie plate, turn over, and remove baking dish. Serve hot with chilled whipped cream.

SERVES 6–8.

Apricot Cheese Rum Tart

CRUST:

Use a 10" baked pastry crust
  (Substitute apricot juice for
  ice water.)

FILLING:

1¼ *cups liquid drained from*
  canned apricot halves
⅓ *cup dark brown sugar,*
  firmly packed
2 *tablespoons cornstarch*
2 *tablespoons butter*
12 *canned apricot halves*
½ *cup thick apricot jam*
2 *3-ounce packages cream*
  cheese
1 *tablespoon dark rum*
1 *cup heavy cream*
2 *teaspoons sugar*
1 *teaspoon dark rum*

Combine apricot juice with brown sugar and cornstarch in saucepan and cook, stirring, until thick and clear. Add the butter and cool slightly, then add the halved apricots and chill. Spread the jam in the bottom of the cooled shell. Combine cheese and rum and beat until light and creamy. Spread over the jam evenly, then spoon on the apricots and chill. Whip the cream with the sugar and rum. To serve, pass the bowl of cream.

SERVES 10–12.

Brownies, Cookies, and Filled Cookies

Apricot Squares
Maple Syrup Brownies
Orange Molasses Squares
Mocha Squares
Lemon Bars
Gingerbread
Brown Sugar Sesame Cookies
Molasses Walnut Cookies
Brown Sugar Almond Cookies
Chocolate-Coated Hazelnut Cookies
Lime Drop Cookies
Miss Grimble's Profiteroles
Sicilian Cream Puffs
Individual Meringues

Apricot Squares

A very popular fruit square that's baked in two layers. Be sure to start the apricots for the topping before you make the base, so they can cool.

8" × 8" pan, buttered

BASE:
1 stick butter
⅓ cup sugar
1 cup all-purpose flour, sifted
½ teaspoon vanilla

Preheat oven to 350°F.
    Cream the butter with the sugar, add the flour and the vanilla, blending well, then press into the bottom of the pan. Bake for 20 minutes.

TOPPING:
⅔ cup chopped dried apricots
2 eggs beaten
1 cup dark brown sugar, packed
⅓ cup all-purpose flour, sifted
½ teaspoon baking powder
¼ teaspoon salt
½ cup chopped walnuts
½ teaspoon vanilla
Confectioners' sugar

Boil the apricots for about ten minutes in water to cover, drain, and cool.
    Combine the eggs with the brown sugar and beat until light.
    Sift the flour, baking powder, and salt and add to the egg mixture. Add apricots, nuts, and vanilla. Blend mixture and spread evenly over base. Return to oven and bake about 30–35 minutes. Cool. Cut into squares and dust with confectioners' sugar.
YIELD: 16 SQUARES.

Maple Syrup Brownies

A good variation on the old theme for maple lovers.

9" × 9" × 2" pan, lightly oiled
2 eggs
¾ cup sugar
1 teaspoon vanilla
½ cup maple syrup—the real stuff
2 ounces bitter chocolate
6 tablespoons butter
¾ cup all-purpose flour
½ teaspoon baking powder
½ cup chopped walnuts
Confectioners' sugar

Preheat oven to 350°F.
    Beat eggs with sugar and vanilla. Add syrup and blend. Melt the chocolate with the butter, remove from heat and slowly blend into egg mixture. Combine dry ingredients and add to maple mixture with chopped walnuts. Spread batter into prepared pan and bake for 25–30 minutes, until the top springs back when touched. When cool, dust with confectioners' sugar and cut into about 24 squares.

Orange Molasses Squares

It must be obvious by now that I am fond of oranges combined with chocolate. I use this combination wherever I can.

10" × 12" pan, lined with
    wax paper
3 eggs
1½ cups dark brown sugar,
    packed
1½ cups flour
1½ teaspoons cinnamon
½ teaspoon ground clove
¼ teaspoon allspice
½ teaspoon baking soda
¼ cup unsulphured molasses
2½ ounces bitter chocolate,
    grated
½ cup chopped orange rind
1¼ cups chopped pecans or
    almonds

Preheat oven to 350°F.

Beat the eggs until light and lemony; add the sugar and blend well. Sift the flour before measuring and resift with all dry ingredients. Add to sugar mixture alternately with molasses. Mix thoroughly; add grated chocolate, orange rind, and nuts. Mix well and spread in pan. Bake in oven until cake begins to leave sides of pan. Cool.

ICING:
1½ cups powdered sugar
1–2 tablespoons cream
Bourbon whiskey

Combine sugar and cream and beat well. Add whiskey slowly, beating steadily until of spreading consistency. Ice cake and cut into 30 2" squares.
SERVES 18–20.

Mocha Squares

Another delightful dessert from the kitchen of my friend Fan Wiener.

13" × 9" pan, greased and
  floured
3 squares bitter chocolate
2 tablespoons instant Sanka®
  coffee
1 stick butter, softened
½ cup Crisco
2 cups sugar
4 eggs
1 teaspoon vanilla
1½ cups cake flour, sifted
1 teaspoon baking powder
½ teaspoon salt
1½ cups chopped walnuts

Preheat oven to 350°F.

Melt chocolate in top of double boiler; add coffee and cool. Cream the butter with the Crisco, add the sugar and beat well, then add the coffee mixture. When blended, beat in the eggs, one at a time, and the vanilla. Sift the dry ingredients and fold into batter with the chopped walnuts. Spread in prepared pan and bake for 35–40 minutes, until top springs back when touched. Cool.

ICING:
4 tablespoons butter
2 cups sifted confectioners'
  sugar
3 tablespoons light cream
1 teaspoon vanilla

Heat butter and brown lightly. Beat in confectioners' sugar, light cream, and vanilla. Spread over cooled cake. Cut into squares and enjoy!
YIELD: 18–20 SQUARES.

Lemon Bars

Those of you who like your desserts more sweet than tart may want to use more sugar in the fruit topping—up to double the amount listed.

8″ × 8″ pan

BASE:
1 cup all-purpose flour
1 stick butter, softened
¼ cup confectioners' sugar

TOPPING:
½ cup sugar
2 tablespoons all-purpose flour
½ teaspoon baking powder
2 beaten eggs
4 tablespoons fresh lemon juice
1 cup chopped pecans
Confectioners' sugar

Preheat oven to 350°F.

Cream together the flour, butter, and confectioners' sugar, and press into pan. Bake in preheated oven for 15 minutes. Remove from oven but leave heat at 350°F.

Mix together the sugar, flour, baking powder, eggs, and lemon juice. Sprinkle the pecans over the cooked base while it's still hot, and pour the egg batter over all. Bake for 20–25 minutes.

Cool. Sprinkle with confectioners' sugar after cutting into squares.
YIELD: 16 SQUARES.

Gingerbread

Another old-fashioned dessert, but still welcome.

8″ × 8″ pan, buttered
½ cup vegetable shortening
½ cup dark brown sugar
1 egg, beaten
½ cup dark molasses
½ cup boiling water
1½ cups all-purpose flour, sifted
1 teaspoon baking soda
1½ teaspoons ginger
1 teaspoon cinnamon
1 teaspoon nutmeg
⅛ teaspoon salt
1 tablespoon orange zest
⅓ cup raisins

Preheat oven to 350°F.

Cream the shortening with the sugar, then add the beaten egg and blend. Combine molasses with hot water.

Resift flour with dry ingredients and add alternately to the butter mixture with molasses. Beat until well blended, add orange zest and raisins and pour into prepared pan. Bake for 25–30 minutes.
SERVES 8.

Brown Sugar Sesame Cookies

A crunchy snap that keeps well.

Cookie sheet, lined with
  waxed paper
½ cup sesame seeds
12 tablespoons butter
1½ cups dark brown sugar,
  packed
2 eggs
1¼ teaspoons vanilla
1¼ cups all-purpose flour,
  sifted
¼ teaspoon salt
¼ teaspoon baking powder
½ teaspoon cinnamon

Preheat oven to 325°F.

While preparing cookie mix, toast sesame seeds by placing in skillet and into a 325°F oven, stirring once in a while so as to brown evenly. Remove from oven when lightly brown.

Cream butter with brown sugar until light. Beat in the eggs and the vanilla.

Sift the dry ingredients together, add toasted sesame seeds and add to the cookie batter, blending thoroughly. Drop by teaspoonfuls about 2 inches apart on waxed paper. Bake 20–25 minutes until lightly brown. Remove from paper while hot.

YIELD: ABOUT 60–70 COOKIES.

Molasses Walnut Cookies

Old-fashioned, inexpensive, and good!

Cookie sheet, buttered
8 tablespoons butter
¾ cup sugar
1 egg
1½ cups all-purpose flour
¾ teaspoon baking soda
Pinch salt
⅓ cup dark molasses
¾ cup chopped walnuts

Preheat oven to 350°F.

Cream the butter with the sugar, add the egg and beat until light.

Sift the flour with the dry ingredients and add to the batter alternately with the molasses. Blend well, then mix in the chopped walnuts. Drop by teaspoonfuls, about 2 inches apart, onto the cookie sheet and bake in preheated oven for 15 minutes.

YIELD: ABOUT 60 COOKIES.

Brown Sugar Almond Cookies

During the twenties and thirties the Adolphus Hotel in Dallas, Texas, boasted a marvelous chef by the name of Georg Vilfordi. My Aunt Mary was the assistant manager of the hotel and one of Georg's admirers. The following is his recipe for the marvelous crisp cookies that Aunt Mary would bring home. The dough freezes beautifully.

Unbuttered cookie sheets
1 stick butter
½ cup dark brown sugar, packed
½ cup sugar
1½ teaspoons instant coffee
2 eggs
¼ teaspoon almond extract, optional
2 cups all-purpose flour
1½ teaspoons cinnamon
½ teaspoon ginger
¼ teaspoon salt
½ teaspoon baking soda
1½ cups sliced blanched almonds

Preheat oven to 375°F.

In an electric mixer cream the butter with the two sugars and coffee. Beat in the eggs and flavoring until smooth. Sift flour with spices, salt, and baking soda, and gradually add to the mixture. Batter will be thick. Lastly add the almonds and blend well. Scrape the batter onto waxed paper and shape into a long roll about 2–2½" in diameter. Cover with additional waxed paper and freeze.

To bake, remove from freezer and, with a very sharp knife, slice in ¼" thick rounds. Bake on cookie sheet in preheated oven 10–12 minutes. MAKES ABOUT 4 DOZEN.

Chocolate-Coated Hazelnut Cookies

A great favorite in Austria and Hungary—and in the Hirsch household, too.

Cookie sheets, buttered
1½ cups flour
¼ teaspoon cinnamon
½ teaspoon cocoa
1½ sticks sweet butter
1 teaspoon grated lemon peel
½ teaspoon lemon juice
¾ cup confectioners' sugar
½ cup ground hazelnuts
¼ cup apricot or strawberry jam
¾ pound semisweet chocolate, melted
¼ cup whole blanched almonds

Preheat oven to 350°F.

Sift flour, cinnamon, and cocoa. Cream butter with lemon peel and juice, and gradually add confectioners' sugar, creaming until fluffy. Blend in ground nuts. Add dry ingredients gradually, mixing until well blended. Cover dough in bowl and wait about 15 minutes to let the flavorings set. Roll dough out on lightly floured board to ¼" thick. Cut cookies with cookie cutter and bake in oven for about 15 minutes. When cookies are cool, turn one-half of them upside down and spread ½ teaspoon of jam on each. Cover with other cookies, sandwich-style. Cover with melted chocolate and decorate each with an almond.

MAKES 2 DOZEN.

Lime Drop Cookies

The flavor of these cookies can be changed to orange or lemon, or a combination of both, by varying the juice and zest used.

Cookie sheet, buttered
8 tablespoons butter, softened
1 cup sugar
1 egg
1 egg yolk
1½ cups all-purpose flour, sifted
1 teaspoon baking powder
½ teaspoon salt
¼ cup fresh lime juice
1 teaspoon lime zest
½ teaspoon lemon zest

Preheat oven to 350°F.

Cream the butter, add sugar, egg, and yolk and blend well.

Sift the dry ingredients together and add to the batter alternately with lime juice, beating to mix. Add zest of lime and lemon, mix again, then drop by teaspoonfuls onto cookie sheet. Bake in preheated oven for 12–15 minutes.

YIELD: ABOUT 75 COOKIES.

Miss Grimble's Profiteroles

Profiteroles are little puff pastries that are filled with your favorite flavored cream or ice cream, then served with your favorite sauce. These were prepared by the dozens for Valentino's showing at Lord & Taylor's more than once.

Cookie sheet, buttered
2 tablespoons butter
1 cup water
Pinch salt
1 tablespoon sugar
1¼ cups all-purpose flour, sifted
5 eggs

Preheat oven to 375°F.

Combine butter and water in a heavy saucepan and bring to a boil. Add salt, sugar, and flour all at once. Remove from heat and stir until mixture leaves the sides of the pan and forms a ball. Cool a little, then add 4 eggs, one at a time, beating to blend. Chill for about 1 hour. Beat the remaining egg and set aside. Drop teaspoonfuls of dough on the prepared cookie sheet about 1" apart. Bake in preheated oven for 20 minutes, then reduce heat to 300°F and continue to bake an additional 5 minutes. Puffs should be golden brown and firm. Remove to a rack and cut small slit in top to allow steam to escape. Slice off the top and fill, then cover and serve.

FILLINGS:
Vanilla, chocolate, or coffee ice cream or
Blend
1 cup heavy cream, whipped, with
2 tablespoons confectioners' sugar and
2 teaspoons Kahlua, Grand Marnier, or curaçao.

When filled, dust with confectioners' sugar, place on serving platter, and pass a bowl of hot fudge sauce. Delightfully decadent!
YIELD: 12 LARGE OR 35 2" PUFFS.

Sicilian Cream Puffs

This special dessert is served on St. Joseph's Day, the religious festival of the patron saint of the home and family. The base is comparable to that for profiteroles. Use the profiterole recipe and add 2 teaspoons grated orange zest and 1 teaspoon grated lemon zest with the sugar and flour.

FILLING:

1 pound of ricotta cheese, sieved

4 tablespoons extra fine granulated sugar

2 tablespoons bitter chocolate, grated

2 tablespoons grated orange zest

1½ teaspoons almond extract

Milk or cream, if needed

Candied orange peel and candied cherries for garnish

Combine the cheese with the sugar and beat until smooth. Fold in the balance of the ingredients. Add cream or milk only if needed to thin. Fill the puffs, dust with powdered sugar, and garnish with thinly sliced candied orange peel and candied cherries.

FILLING FOR 1½ DOZEN.

Individual Meringues

These are the darlings of the schaumtorte world! Easy to prepare, they lend themselves to any filling. Try my rendition.

Cookie sheet, buttered
4 egg whites, room temperature
1⅓ cups sugar
½ teaspoon cream of tartar
1 cup chestnut purée, unsweetened (Faugier brand)
½ cup sugar
½ cup grated semisweet chocolate
1 tablespoon grated orange zest
1 package frozen raspberries, defrosted
1 cup heavy cream, whipped and lightly sweetened

Preheat oven to 275°F.

Beat egg whites until stiff, then slowly beat in the sugar and cream of tartar. Continue to beat until egg whites are thick, smooth, and glossy.

With a spoon, shape 16 rounds on the cookie sheet with a slight well in each. Bake in oven for 35–40 minutes. They should be a pale brown. Turn off the heat and let cool in the oven to room temperature. Remove from cookie sheet.

Combine purée with sugar, grated chocolate, and orange zest. When ready to serve, spread filling on 8 meringues, top with other 8, and pass bowl of defrosted raspberries for topping along with bowl of lightly sweetened whipped cream!
SERVES 8.

Tree of Life Desserts

Supreme Baked Apples
Vermont Baked Apples
Baked Bananas with Rum
Boozey Berry Flambé
Figs in Cream
Flambéed Fresh Purple Figs
Grapes in Cream
Broiled Grapefruit Elegant
Frozen Orange Cups
Fresh Peach Delicacies
Peaches with Marsala
Hurry-Up Peach Melba
Champagne Peaches
Pears Amandine
Italian Pears in Wine
Caramel Pears
Barcelona Pineapple Flambé
Pineapple Rum Flambé
Strawberries in Raspberry Cream
Brandied Strawberries with Crème Fraîche
Honeyed Fruit Cointreau
Marinated Fresh Fruit with Sherbet and Champagne

Supreme Baked Apples

12" × 8" × 2" glass baking
  dish
6 medium to large Rome baking apples
¼ cup raisins
½ cup Cointreau
⅓ cup chopped walnuts
½ cup dark brown sugar

Preheat oven to 375°F.

Wash and core the apples to about ½" of the bottom. Marinate the raisins in 3 tablespoons of the liqueur for 1–2 hours.

Combine raisins, soaking liqueur, walnuts, and sugar, and fill apples. Add a tablespoon of liqueur to each apple. Set the apples into a flat glass baking dish, into which pour ¾ cup hot water and a tablespoon of the liqueur. Bake, basting once in a while, until done, about an hour. Cool in pan, continuing to baste.

Serve at room temperature with the juices spooned over.

SERVES 6.

Vermont Baked Apples

This is the simplest and one of the best baked apple recipes I've ever seen.

8" × 8" baking dish
4 medium to large Rome
  baking apples
2 tablespoons grated lemon
  zest
¾ cup pure maple syrup

Preheat oven to 375°F.

Wash and core the apples to about ½" of the bottom, and place in glass baking dish. Spoon zest into apples and pour maple syrup in and over apples. Bake for about 1 hour, basting frequently with the syrup. Delicious warm or cold.

SERVES 4.

Baked Bananas with Rum

Sometimes in the winter our Sunday brunch was enhanced with this delightful finale. My husband liked this topped with sweetened whipped cream or vanilla ice cream.

12" × 8" × 2" glass baking
  dish, buttered
1 cup light brown sugar,
  packed
¾ teaspoon cinnamon
¼ teaspoon cloves
½ cup chopped pecans or walnuts (optional)
8 small bananas, peeled
1 8-ounce can crushed
  pineapple with juice
¼ cup dark rum
4 tablespoons butter

Preheat oven to 350°F.

Combine sugar, spices, and nuts. Arrange bananas in buttered dish, add spice mixture, then pineapple with juice and rum. Dot with butter and bake 30–35 minutes, until bananas are fork tender. During the baking, spoon the sauce over the top.
SERVES 6–8.

Boozey Berry Flambé

The variation in liqueur is up to you. I have used kirschwasser, Cointreau, curaçao, and Grand Marnier with equal success.

Chafing dish
2½ tablespoons sugar
2 tablespoons fresh orange
  juice—save the rind
1 2–3-inch piece of orange
  rind
1 2–3-inch piece of lemon
  rind
½ cup your favorite liqueur
10-ounce box frozen raspberries or sliced strawberries,
  defrosted
1 quart vanilla ice cream

In a chafing dish on low heat, combine the sugar, orange juice, and rinds, stirring until sugar is dissolved. Add 5 tablespoons of liqueur chosen and the berries.

Warm a ladle and pour into it last 3 tablespoons of liqueur, and set ablaze. When flame dies out, pour over berry mixture and serve over ice cream.

VARIATION:
Whir defrosted fruits in a blender and double the other ingredients.

SERVES 8.

Figs in Cream

We always had fig trees in our backyards. Fresh figs were always abundant, if you could get them before the birds! Aside from serving them fresh, or preserving them, this is an unusual and welcome variation.

3–4 tablespoons cognac
12–18 ripe green figs, pierced
1 cup sour cream
6 tablespoons Grand Marnier
    or curaçao

Sprinkle the cognac over the figs and allow to stand at room temperature for 1–2 hours.
    Combine the sour cream with the Grand Marnier or curaçao and pour over the figs. Chill before serving.
SERVES 6–8.

Flambéed Fresh Purple Figs

If you are as fond of fresh purple figs as I am, you will like this idea.

Chafing dish or heavy skillet
1 dozen ripe purple figs,
    peeled
3 tablespoons curaçao
3 tablespoons brandy
1 cup heavy cream

Place the figs in a chafing dish or heavy skillet over medium heat. Combine the two liqueurs and pour over the figs. Ignite, and while there is a flame, prick each fig several times, shaking the pan until the flame dies. Serve immediately with a cold pitcher of heavy cream.
SERVES 6.

Grapes in Cream

This is an old favorite.

2½–3 pounds green seedless
    grapes, washed and dried
¾–1 cup dark brown sugar
2 cups sour cream

Combine all and refrigerate overnight.
SERVES 6.

Broiled Grapefruit Elegant

In the mid-thirties, my father became the owner of a citrus grove in Harlingen, Texas, in exchange for monies loaned and not returned. My mother prepared grapefruit in as many ways as she could devise, aside from having them for breakfast daily! The following was one of the best. I still serve it.

1 grapefruit, at room temperature

Dark brown sugar

2 tablespoons apricot brandy

Butter

Preheat broiler.

Halve and section the grapefruit. Spread each half generously with dark brown sugar, about ⅛" thick. Pour 1 tablespoon apricot brandy over each half and let stand about 30 minutes. Before broiling, dot the tops with slivers of butter and broil until nicely brown and the sugar forms a slight glaze. Serve immediately.

SERVES 2.

Frozen Orange Cups

4 large navel oranges

⅓ cup curaçao

1 quart lemon sherbet

Cut oranges in half and gently remove the segments. Remove and discard all the pith from the shells and freeze. Pour liqueur over reserved orange segments and marinate for about 1 hour.

Soften the sherbet just enough to blend with about 6 tablespoons of the marinade. Quickly fill the frozen orange shells, mounding the tops. Freeze.

To serve, decorate tops with the reserved marinated orange sections.

SERVES 8.

Fresh Peach Delicacies

Very continental.

Chafing dish
1 cup sugar
1 cup water
Zest of 1 lemon
4 peaches, peeled, halved,
    and pitted
4 tablespoons butter
½ cup raspberries, crushed
Juice of 1 orange
4–5 ounces kirschwasser or
    brandy
2–3 ounces curaçao or Coin-
    treau or Grand Marnier
1 quart vanilla ice cream

Combine sugar, water, and lemon zest in sauce-pan and heat. When sugar is dissolved, poach the peaches about 10 minutes.

Remove from syrup with slotted spoon. Reserve ½ cup of poaching syrup.

Light a chafing dish and in it combine butter, raspberries, orange juice, and reserved poaching syrup. Stir for a few minutes, and, when hot, place peaches in dish, cut side down. Baste with the sauce for a few minutes.

In a small saucepan heat kirsch or brandy and curaçao or Cointreau or Grand Marnier. Pour heated liqueurs over peaches and flambé.

Serve a peach on scoop of vanilla ice cream and spoon sauce over the top.
SERVES 8.

Peaches with Marsala

2 cups sugar
2 cups water
½ teaspoon vanilla
6 peaches, peeled, halved,
    and pitted
6 egg yolks
½ cup sugar
½ cup marsala wine
1 quart ice cream
Chopped pistachios for garnish

Combine sugar, water, and vanilla, and boil for 10 minutes. Add peaches and poach for about 10 minutes. Remove with slotted spoon and cool.

In the top of a double boiler over hot water beat until light egg yolks and sugar. Then add marsala.

Beat the sauce until thick, then spoon into chilled bowl and continue to beat over ice until cold. Chill.

Serve a peach on top of a scoop of ice cream and spoon the sauce over the top. Garnish with chopped pistachios.
SERVES 12.

Hurry-Up Peach Melba

This is a life-saver when unexpected guests arrive for dinner besides being delicious. If fresh peaches are available, they are preferable. If not, the firmest canned peaches will suffice.

2 10-ounce packages frozen
    raspberries in syrup, de-
    frosted
Juice of 1 lemon
⅔ cup Cointreau
8 peach halves
Vanilla ice cream

Purée raspberries with syrup, lemon juice, and Cointreau in blender. Place peach halves on top of scoops of vanilla ice cream and top with melba sauce.
SERVES 8.

Champagne Peaches

Give your guests their just desserts! This is both dessert and after-dinner drink, and best when fresh peaches are plentiful. An elegant finale to any dinner.

Spoon 1 teaspoon of peach brandy into each chilled wine glass. Add to each glass ½ of a peeled fresh peach. Pierce the peach all over with a fork. Fill the wine glass with chilled champagne and serve.

Pears Amandine

1 cup water
½ cup sugar
⅛ teaspoon vanilla
3 fresh Anjou pears, peeled, halved, and cored
¼ cup slivered toasted almonds
1 cup sliced strawberries, with their juice
1 cup heavy cream, whipped

Combine the water and sugar in a saucepan and boil for 3–4 minutes. Add the vanilla and the pears and cook slowly for 6–8 minutes, only until fork tender.

Place pear halves, round side up, on a serving platter and decorate by sticking toasted almond slivers into the pears.

Reduce remaining syrup by one-half, add the strawberries and their juice, and boil the mixture again to a thick syrup. Pour all in a blender, or force through a sieve, then spoon over the pears and chill until serving time. Pass the whipped cream.

SERVES 6.

Italian Pears in Wine

My first introduction to pears prepared in this manner was in 1960 on my first visit to Rome. We lunched at Tre Scalini in the Piazza Novona. The day was beautiful, and so was the company and the lunch.

Warm, these are a wonderful side dish for a rib roast.

4 cups water
1 cup dry white wine
1½ cups sugar
2 lemons, juice and rind
1 tablespoon grated orange peel
8 Bosc pears, peeled

Place all ingredients in a large saucepan and bring to a boil. Reduce heat, cover, and continue to simmer until pears are fork tender—about 30 minutes, turning to cook evenly. Remove pears to a serving bowl and reduce juices to about two cups. Discard rind. Pour syrup over pears, cool to room temperature, cover and refrigerate.

SERVES 8.

Caramel Pears

When Anjou pears are in season, be sure to try this dessert.

10" shallow baking dish
6 firm Anjou pears, peeled, quartered, and cored
½ cup sugar
4 tablespoons butter
¾–1 cup heavy cream, at room temperature

Preheat oven to 550°F.

Arrange the pears closely packed in the baking dish. Sprinkle with the sugar and dot with the butter. Bake in preheated oven until sugar is brown and caramelized. Add the heavy cream. Spoon the caramelized juice and the cream over the pears to blend the sauce. Serve warm.
SERVES 6.

Barcelona Pineapple Flambé

On a trip to Spain in 1974, our last stop was Barcelona, and our last night's dinner was at a divine restaurant named Oratanas. The dessert was prepared at the table, and I have since successfully duplicated it at home.

1 ripe pineapple, freshly sliced
Brown sugar
1 scoop vanilla ice cream
1½ ounces White Horse scotch

Use two slices of pineapple per person, separating them on the plate. Lightly sprinkle with brown sugar, top with vanilla ice cream and White Horse scotch. Ignite and flambé until the blue flame dies. Only White Horse can be used to obtain this wonderful flavor!
SERVES 1.

Pineapple Rum Flambé

This is the pièce de résistance over fresh pineapple slices but could double as a crêpe topping. Would top 8–10 crêpes, to serve 4–6.

Cast-iron skillet
4 tablespoons sweet butter
4 tablespoons sugar
Juice of 2 large oranges
Zest of 1 orange
4 slices pineapple, diced, preferably fresh
4 bananas, peeled, halved, and quartered
4 tablespoons crème de banana liqueur
4 tablespoons dark Jamaica rum
1 fresh pineapple, peeled, cored, and sliced
1 quart vanilla ice cream

Melt butter, add sugar, and heat until caramelized. Add orange juice and zest and simmer 3–4 minutes. Add diced pineapple, bananas, and banana liqueur. Heat thoroughly, then add the rum and flambé. Serve over fresh pineapple slices, topped with vanilla ice cream.
SERVES 4–6.

Strawberries in Raspberry Cream

Don't miss this treat when both berries are in season.

⅓ cup sugar
1 pint fresh strawberries, washed, stemmed, and drained
⅓ cup orange juice
2 tablespoons kirschwasser
½ pint fresh raspberries, washed and drained
¼ cup confectioners' sugar
1½ cups heavy cream, whipped

Sprinkle the sugar over the strawberries. Add the orange juice and kirschwasser. Cover and chill for several hours. Purée the raspberries, add the confectioners' sugar, and fold into the whipped cream. Serve over the strawberries.
SERVES 6.

Brandied Strawberries with Crème Fraîche

What a wonderful do-ahead summer dessert!

3 pints strawberries, washed,
    stemmed, and drained
⅓ cup sugar
3 tablespoons cherry brandy
1 cup crème fraîche
½ cup pistachio nuts, chopped

CRÈME FRAÎCHE:
1 teaspoon buttermilk
1 cup heavy cream

Combine the strawberries with the sugar and cherry brandy. Marinate in the refrigerator several hours, tossing once in a while. Serve in individual bowls and top with a dollop of crème fraîche. Sprinkle with the pistachio nuts.
SERVES 6–8.

Mix the buttermilk and the heavy cream together in a glass jar. Cover and let stand for 6–8 hours at 75°. Stir. Then refrigerate until needed.
YIELDS APPROXIMATELY 1 CUP.

Honeyed Fruit Cointreau

Large, shallow baking dish
1 can peaches, halved and
    quartered, reserve syrup
1 can halved apricots, pitted
    and drained
2 apples, peeled, cored, and
    cut into eighths
1 fresh pineapple, peeled,
    cored, and cut into cubes
3 oranges, peeled and cut into
    sections
3 grapefruits, peeled and sec-
    tioned
½ cup honey
¼ cup Cointreau or Grand
    Marnier
Zest of 1 orange, grated (ap-
    proximately 2 tablespoons)
Juice of 1 lemon

Preheat oven to 350°F.
  In a baking dish, marinate all fruit in honey and Cointreau, with peach syrup and zest and lemon juice. Let stand for an hour. Bake for 25 minutes. Cool to room temperature. Serve, with or without sweetened whipped cream.
SERVES 8–10.

Marinated Fresh Fruit with Sherbet and Champagne

This is an easy dessert for a large party as it can all be prepared ahead of time. Increase the quantity of fruit according to the number of guests.

1 fresh pineapple, peeled, cored, and diced

2 bananas, peeled and sliced

2 cups fresh strawberries, washed, stemmed, and drained

2 whole oranges, peeled and sliced in halves

1 cup seedless green grapes

½ cup sugar

¼ cup kirschwasser

1 pint lemon sherbet

1 quart chilled champagne

Combine all the fruit in a large bowl (about 6 quarts) and sprinkle with the sugar and kirschwasser. Toss to cover and taste for flavor. Marinate and chill for several hours. Taste again for flavor. To serve, spoon into glass dessert dishes or tall sherbet glasses and top each with a scoop lemon sherbet and a good splash of chilled champagne. THIS SHOULD SERVE 8–10.

Cooked Desserts

Basic Individual Dessert Crêpes
Applesauce and Rum Dessert Crêpes
Creole Crêpes Praline
Heavenly Cheese Blintzes
Walnut-Rum-Raisin Blintzes
Pineapple Blintzes
French Pancakes à la Ricketts
Chocolate Pancakes
Yogurt Pancakes
Belgian Waffles
Chocolate Waffles
German Flambéed Omelet
Macaroon Omelet

Basic Individual Dessert Crêpes

Everyone should learn how to prepare these crêpes. There are many ways to finish them; they are delicious simply spread with jelly, folded, and dusted with sugar. The recipe given will make 8 to 10, serving three. To double the amount, merely repeat the ingredients.

2 eggs
¾ cup milk
½ cup all-purpose flour plus
  1 tablespoon
1 teaspoon vegetable oil
Pinch salt
1½ teaspoons kirschwasser
1½ teaspoons granulated
  sugar
Additional vegetable oil and
  butter for greasing pan

Put all ingredients except additional vegetable oil and butter in an electric blender for a few seconds. This will give you a perfect batter. Let the batter stand at least one hour before using.

Heat a 6″ frying pan. I prefer a cast-iron Wagner. Grease it with a few drops of vegetable oil and ⅛ teaspoon butter for each crêpe. Pour in 2½ tablespoons of the batter for each crêpe, tipping pan to spread evenly. Cook over moderate heat until bottom is lightly browned and the top is dry. Turn and brown the other side. Invert crêpe on a dish towel. Continue until all the batter is used.
SERVES 3.

Applesauce and Rum Dessert Crêpes

Use the recipe for the Basic Individual Dessert Crêpes (p. 115) substituting rum for kirschwasser. These are quite unusual.

Heatproof platter, buttered
Make 24 thin crêpes—6″
  each (triple the recipe)
2½ cups natural applesauce
3 tablespoons brown sugar
2 teaspoons grated lemon zest
Dash nutmeg
1 tablespoon butter
Extra-fine granulated sugar
¼ cup rum, warmed

Preheat oven 400°F.

In a saucepan, combine the applesauce with the sugar, lemon zest, nutmeg, and butter, and simmer until it is quite thick and lightly browned. Spread on crêpes, roll up, and place on buttered heatproof platter. Dust with the extra fine sugar and glaze in preheated oven for a few minutes.

Remove to serving platter, sprinkle with warmed rum and ignite. Serve as soon as flame dies.
SERVES 6–8.

Creole Crêpes Praline

This is a recipe from the Praline Liqueur company. As we all know, peaches lend themselves beautifully to a brown sugar base, such as praline, so give these a whirl for Sunday brunch!

8" skillet

CRÊPES:
3 eggs
3 egg yolks
½ cup milk
½ cup water
2 tablespoons butter, melted
2 tablespoons Praline liqueur
1 cup all-purpose flour
½ teaspoon salt
Additional butter for greasing
   pan

Whirl all ingredients except additional butter in a blender until smooth. Let batter stand at room temperature for at least 1 hour. Cook crêpes in a buttered skillet, using 4 tablespoons batter for each crêpe, and cook both sides of the crêpe until golden. Turn out on dish towel.

Stack the crêpes between sheets of waxed paper until serving. Crêpes may be made ahead of time and warmed before serving.

SAUCE:
3 tablespoons butter
¾ cup peach preserves
2½ tablespoons honey
½ cup Praline liqueur

Melt the butter in a skillet. Over low heat combine peach preserves and honey with butter. Place a crêpe in the skillet and turn gently to coat both sides lightly. Fold the crêpe in half once, then in half again to form a quarter circle. Pick up with tongs, draining excess sauce into skillet. Repeat with remaining crêpes. Keep warm. Warm Praline liqueur slowly and pour over crêpes. Ignite carefully and enjoy!
SERVES 4.

Heavenly Cheese Blintzes

Always a special treat in our house were Mother's cheese blintzes. We were served these for dessert with sour cream or homemade strawberry preserves, or both if you were so inclined, and most of the time we were!

This recipe only serves 4—so go to work! And be sure to try out all the sauces.

PANCAKE BATTER:
3 eggs, well beaten
⅔ cup water
½ cup plus 2 tablespoons all-purpose flour
¼ teaspoon salt
2 tablespoons confectioners' sugar
Melted butter

Blend all except butter until smooth. Heat a 6″ skillet, brush with melted butter. Add a small bit of the batter, tipping the skillet to let the batter cover the entire pan, pour residue back into reserved batter. Cook over moderate heat until top is set and bubbly. Invert pan on tea towel.

Continue until all batter is used, always brushing the pan anew before each blintz is made.

FILLING:
12 ounces dry cottage cheese or farmers cheese
1 egg
⅛ teaspoon salt
3 tablespoons sugar
3 tablespoons cream may be added if cheese mixture is too dry
Butter

Mix all except butter until smooth and place 2–3 tablespoons a little off center on each pancake. Fold into square pocket: Fold the bottom of the pancake up, fold in the sides, then fold over the top.

Butter a large skillet and fry blintzes until golden brown on both sides. Serve hot.
SERVES 4.

Walnut-Rum-Raisin Blintzes

Top this blintz with melted semisweet chocolate, flavored with rum to taste.

PANCAKE BATTER:
1 recipe pancake batter for Heavenly Cheese Blintzes

Prepare pancakes according to directions (see p. 117) and set aside.

FILLING:
1 recipe filling for Heavenly Cheese Blintzes
¼ cup ground walnuts
1 tablespoon rum
½ cup white raisins
1 tablespoon grated orange zest

Prepare filling for Heavenly Cheese Blintzes (see p. 117) and blend in remaining ingredients, keeping butter aside. Place 2–3 tablespoons of filling a little off center on each pancake. Fold into square pocket: Fold the bottom of the pancake up, fold in the sides, then fold over the top.

Butter a large skillet and fry blintzes until golden brown on both sides. Serve hot.
SERVES 4.

Apricot and Almond Sauce

Use this sauce with Walnut-Rum-Raisin Blintzes, above. Try adding 2 tablespoons lemon zest to the filling, but bake the blintzes instead of frying them.

¾ cup thick apricot jam
¼ cup fresh orange juice
2 tablespoons melted butter
1 tablespoon lemon juice
2 teaspoons lemon zest
2 tablespoons chopped toasted almonds, pecans, or walnuts

Blend all the ingredients together in a bowl. Spoon some of the sauce over the blintzes in a buttered heatproof baking dish and bake for 8–10 minutes at 350°–375°F. Serve with additional sauce that's been heated in a pan.
SERVES 8.

Best-Ever Sauce

Here's another topper for Heavenly Cheese Blintzes (see p. 117) or Walnut-Rum-Raisin Blintzes. Bake—don't fry—the blintzes.

1 stick butter, melted
4 tablespoons brandy
4 tablespoons curaçao or Grand Marnier
2–3 tablespoons lemon juice

Blend all ingredients together in a bowl. Spoon some of the sauce over blintzes in a heatproof baking dish and bake for 8–10 minutes at 350°–375°F. Serve with additional sauce that's been gently heated in a pan.
SERVES 8.

Pineapple Blintzes

Try dusting these with sugar, a dash of powdered ginger, and your choice of chopped nuts. Then dot with butter and bake as directed. Or really go all the way and use the Pineapple Sauce.

PANCAKE BATTER:
1 recipe pancake batter for
  Heavenly Cheese Blintzes

Prepare pancakes according to directions (see p. 117) and set aside.

FILLING:
1 recipe filling for Heavenly
  Cheese Blintzes
½ cup drained pineapple

Prepare filling for Heavenly Cheese Blintzes (see p. 117) and blend in the pineapple. Fill and fold pancakes. Arrange in a buttered heatproof baking dish.

PINEAPPLE SAUCE:
4–6 tablespoons butter
1 cup sugar
2 eggs
2 egg yolks
Juice of one whole lemon and
  the grated rind
1 can crushed pineapple,
  drained
Brown sugar, sifted

Melt butter in the top of a double boiler with the sugar and whole eggs beaten with the yolks, lemon juice, and grated rind. Cook, stirring constantly, until thickened. Remove from heat.

When cool, fold in the drained pineapple, as much as you like, to thicken. Spoon over the blintzes in the pan, dust with sifted brown sugar, and bake in 350°F oven for 8–10 minutes.
SERVES 4.

My final word on blintz toppings is *improvise!*

French Pancakes à la Ricketts

The summer I was fifteen, I was permitted to visit my older cousins in Chicago before entering the university the following fall. Our favorite hangout before turning in for the evening was a café called Ricketts, where Sophie Tucker was performing. We only ordered one dish each time—French pancakes with hot strawberry preserves, dusted with confectioners' sugar. This is so divine you must try it. It was a frequent Sunday night request by husband and children. A good accompaniment: sausages, hot and crisp, or thin slices of baked ham.

BATTER:
3 eggs, well-beaten
⅔ cup water, or half water and half milk
½ cup all-purpose flour plus 2 tablespoons
¼ teaspoon salt
2 tablespoons confectioners' sugar
Melted butter

Blend all except butter until smooth. Heat a 6″ skillet and brush with melted butter. Add a small amount of the batter, tipping the pan to let the batter cover the entire skillet, and pour off residue into reserved batter. Cook over moderate heat. When brown on the bottom, turn pancake over and brown the other side. Invert pan on tea towel.

FILLING:

Place homemade strawberry preserves or the best commercial variety in top of double boiler to keep hot. Spoon 2–3 tablespoons on each pancake, roll up, and dust with confectioners' sugar. SERVES 4.

Chocolate Pancakes

A good dessert after a light supper.

2 eggs, separated
1 tablespoon butter
2 tablespoons cocoa
¾ teaspoon salt
1¼ tablespoons sugar
1 cup milk plus 2 tablespoons
1½ cups flour
1½ teaspoons baking powder
Additional butter
Powdered sugar

Combine egg yolks with butter and beat until light. Add cocoa, salt, sugar, and 2 tablespoons milk. Sift flour before measuring, and resift with baking powder. Add flour to mixture alternately with 1 cup milk. Beat egg whites until stiff and fold into the batter gently.

Melt butter in skillet and spoon on batter to make about 3 to 4 6" pancakes. Brown both sides, remove to heated platter, and serve dusted with powdered sugar.

MAKES ABOUT 16–18; SERVES 8–10.

Yogurt Pancakes

I have a dear friend who comes from Beirut, Lebanon. This is her version of pancakes. They are wonderful topped with anything you can devise. Cook them on a hot griddle.

2 eggs, separated
1 cup yogurt
¾ cups all-purpose flour, sifted
1 tablespoon sugar
1 teaspoon baking soda
½ teaspoon salt
8 tablespoons butter, melted

Beat the egg yolks and combine with the yogurt. Add sifted dry ingredients, blend, then add the melted butter.

Beat the egg whites until stiff. Fold in the beaten egg whites. Ladle onto a hot buttered griddle. Cook until bubbles appear. Turn to brown the other side.

SERVES 4.

Belgian Waffles

My college graduation present to my younger daughter, Deborah, was a course at Marcella Hazan's in Bologna. From there I met her in Europe and one of our stops was in the fascinating city of the guilds, Brussels. We grew fatter, but loved every ounce as we enjoyed Belgian waffles for lunch each day in a lovely fast-food restaurant that specialized in this excess!

These were served with lightly sweetened whipped cream, with or without sliced fruit of the season. We were lucky, and fresh fruits of all kinds were in season—peaches, strawberries and raspberries—and the whipped cream was truly thick and creamy!

4 cups flour
Pinch salt
½ cup confectioners' sugar
2 cups water
3 eggs, separated
1 stick sweet butter, softened
2 cups milk

In an electric mixer combine the flour, salt, sugar, water, and egg yolks. Mix well and add the softened butter. Beat until smooth. Add milk and beat again.

Beat egg whites until stiff and fold into mixture. Spoon into heated waffle iron and bake until crisp and brown.

SERVES 8–10.

Chocolate Waffles

1 stick butter
1 cup sugar
2 eggs, separated
½ cup milk
1½ cups all-purpose flour
2 teaspoons baking powder
Pinch salt
2 squares bitter chocolate,
    melted
1 teaspoon vanilla

Cream butter and sugar. Beat the egg yolks well and add with milk. Sift the dry ingredients together and add, followed by the melted chocolate and vanilla. Beat thoroughly. Fold in stiffly beaten whites. Bake in oiled and heated waffle iron and serve with sweetened whipped cream, or chocolate sauce.

CHOCOLATE SAUCE:
2 squares bitter chocolate
⅓ cup hot water
1½ cups sugar
1 tablespoon butter
¾ cup heavy cream
Pinch salt
1 teaspoon vanilla

Melt the chocolate in the water in the top of a double boiler. Add sugar, butter, cream, and salt. Cook for about 10 minutes over low heat. Add vanilla.

This is good served hot or cold. For variety, top with ice cream or powdered sugar.
SERVES 6.

German Flambéed Omelet

This was Mother's specialty for Sunday brunch, especially when we had the USO boys as guests. Serve the omelet with crisp bacon, sausages, or baked ham. If you want a fluffier omelet, separate the eggs, folding the whites in last.

4 eggs
¼ cup milk
½ teaspoon salt
1 tablespoon butter
Granulated sugar
Apricot or peach brandy or
    rum

Beat eggs and add milk and salt. Melt butter in 10″ skillet, and when hot add the eggs. Cook over low heat until bottom is browned. Remove to preheated broiler and continue to cook on lowest level until puffed and brown. Sprinkle with granulated sugar, slip onto a warmed platter and serve immediately with 1 jigger of apricot or peach brandy or rum poured over and flambéed!
SERVES 4.

Macaroon Omelet

A dessert omelet worth the effort.

6 eggs
1 tablespoon cold water
Pinch salt
1 tablespoon butter
3 large almond macaroons,
  crushed
3 tablespoons apple jelly
1 cup heavy cream, whipped
1 tablespoon sugar

Beat the eggs, water, and salt with a fork for several minutes. Melt the butter in a 12″ skillet, coating the pan evenly.

While the butter is melting, prepare the filling by blending the crushed macaroons with the apple jelly and add 1 tablespoon of the whipped cream. Pour the beaten eggs into the hot skillet, reduce heat to moderate, and tip skillet to spread the eggs evenly over the surface. Push the omelet from the sides with a fork to permit the eggs to run to the bottom. Cook until fairly firm, then turn out on an ovenproof dish, add the prepared filling, fold the omelet over, sprinkle with the sugar and glaze briefly under a hot broiler. Serve with the remaining whipped cream.
SERVES 3–4.

Mousses

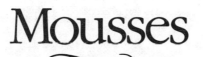

Chocolate Macaroon Mousse
French Mousse
Flambéed Mocha Chocolate Mousse
Molasses Chip Mousse
Chocolate Almond Mousse
Chocolate Mousse with Cognac
Spanish Mousse au Chocolat
Frozen Maple Mousse
Lemon Mousse with White Wine

Chocolate Macaroon Mousse

This mousse always brings raves from family and friends. It really deserves all the praise—as you will see.

10" pie pan, buttered
6–8 almond macaroons, crumbled
½ pound dark sweet chocolate
4–5 tablespoons cold water
5 eggs, separated
2 tablespoons rum
Lightly sweetened whipped cream for garnish

Line pie pan with crumbled macaroons. Melt chocolate and water over low heat, stirring until smooth. Remove from heat and cool slightly.

Beat the egg yolks until light, then carefully and slowly add to the chocolate, along with the rum. Mix well. Beat the egg whites until stiff and fold into mixture, then spoon into prepared pie pan. Refrigerate for at least 4 hours, top with lightly sweetened whipped cream and serve.
SERVES 8–10.

French Mousse

When my children were young, they referred to this favorite as a *chocolate moustache*! I'm certain it's no misnomer as at the end of the meal that's exactly what they had!

The mousse may be garnished with additional whipped cream, chocolate fudge sauce, or maraschino cherries—just let yourself go as long as you have indulged this far!

1 2-quart mold or 6–8 individual molds
3 ounces Maillards sweet chocolate
2 tablespoons extra-strong cold coffee
1 teaspoon instant coffee
4 eggs, separated
½ cup sugar
Pinch salt
1½ cups heavy cream, whipped

Melt the chocolate in the top of a double boiler. Blend in the coffees well, then set aside to cool.

Beat the egg yolks until lemony, add the sugar and salt, and beat again, then add the cooled chocolate mixture and blend thoroughly.

Beat the egg whites until stiff and fold in, and lastly, fold in the whipped cream. Spoon into a 2 quart mold, or individual molds, and chill 2–3 hours.
SERVES 6–8.

Flambéed Mocha Chocolate Mousse

On a trip through Switzerland, my daughter Deborah and I visited Berne. Our dinner the first evening was at the famous Rabbus restaurant. The entire dinner was delightful, but the dessert was extraordinary! This is my adaptation of their most delightful mocha mousse.

CHOCOLATE CUPS:
12 ounces sweet chocolate
16 paper baking cups

Melt chocolate in the top of a double boiler over hot water; remove from heat and cool slightly. While chocolate is cooling, double up paper cups. Put 2 tablespoons of the cooled chocolate in each of the 8 cups. Using the back of a teaspoon, spread the chocolate around the cup so that the entire inside is coated. When all are done, set them in a muffin pan and chill until the chocolate is firm.

FILLING:
4 squares semisweet chocolate
¼ cup double-strength coffee
1½ tablespoons crème de cacao
1 cup heavy cream
¼ cup sugar
Grand Marnier

Melt chocolate with coffee over low heat. Cool, then stir in the liqueur. Whip the cream until it starts to thicken, then gradually add the sugar and continue whipping until stiff. Gently fold into the cooled chocolate mixture. Spoon into prepared chocolate shells and freeze.

To serve, gently peel off the paper cups, invert chocolate cups on plate and spoon 1 tablespoon of Grand Marnier over each. Ignite and serve.
SERVES 8.

Molasses Chip Mousse

We owe the House of Hershey a great vote of thanks! Try this—it is easy and gives great returns for the little it asks.

1 large can Hershey chocolate syrup
1 pound molasses chip candy, crushed
4 cups heavy cream, whipped

Blend the syrup and the crushed candy into the whipped cream. Pour into refrigerator tray and freeze. Cut into squares and serve.
SERVES 8.

Chocolate Almond Mousse

16–20 paper cupcake cups or
  2 refrigerator trays
1 8½-ounce chocolate candy
  bar with almonds
¼ cup water
2 eggs, beaten
2 cups heavy cream, whipped
Additional whipped cream for
  garnish

Break candy bar into pieces, place in top of double boiler with water and melt, stirring to blend. Quickly add the beaten eggs, stirring constantly, and cook over boiling water another 2–3 minutes. Remove from heat and cool slightly.

Fold in the whipped cream and pour into refrigerator trays or paper cupcake cups and freeze quickly (turn freezer to high until mousse is frozen, then return control to normal freezing temperature).

The cups may be decorated with a dollop of whipped cream. The trays can be cut into squares and also decorated.

SERVES 16–20.

Chocolate Mousse with Cognac

The French have a way with desserts enhanced with their favorite beverage—cognac. This one is exceptional.

8 pot de crème cups
4 eggs, separated
¼ cup cognac
½ cup sugar plus 1 tablespoon
6 ounces semisweet chocolate
1 stick butter
1 teaspoon instant coffee, dissolved in ¼ cup hot water

In the top of a double boiler combine the egg yolks with the cognac, and beat well. Add ½ cup sugar and beat again, stirring until thickened—about 10 minutes. Place over cold water and beat 3–4 minutes until cool. Melt the chocolate and the butter together in another saucepan, add the coffee mixture, then add to the egg yolk mixture and blend. Beat the egg whites to peaks with the 1 tablespoon sugar and fold into chocolate mixture. Pour into 8 pot de crème cups. Chill and serve.

SERVES 8.

Spanish Mousse au Chocolat

The origin of this mousse has always been a mystery—what part of Spain—nevertheless, it is delicious. Top with sweetened whipped cream and grated semisweet chocolate—or serve plain.

6 pot de crème cups
½ pound dark sweet chocolate
5 tablespoons strong coffee
5 eggs, separated
2 tablespoons dark rum

Melt the chocolate with the coffee in a double boiler over boiling water. Remove from heat and add egg yolks one by one, stirring constantly, then the rum. Beat whites until stiff and gently fold into chocolate mixture. Pour into pot de crème cups and chill.
SERVES 6.

Frozen Maple Mousse

All Vermonters come to attention. Look what can be made with your delicious syrup!

4–5 cup mold
¾ cup maple syrup
3 egg whites, stiffly beaten
2 cups heavy cream, whipped
Additional heavy cream,
    sweetened and whipped
Toasted slivered almonds

Cook maple syrup to the crack stage, 270°F. Pour very slowly in a steady stream over beaten egg whites, beating egg whites constantly. Cool.

Fold in the whipped heavy cream and spoon into mold. Freeze. Top with additional lightly sweetened whipped cream and toasted almonds.
SERVES 8.

MOUSSES

Lemon Mousse with White Wine

This is a perfect dessert after a heavy dinner.

1 tablespoon gelatin
2 tablespoons water
¼ cup sweet white wine
½ cup granulated sugar
Juice and zest of 1½ large
  lemons
4 eggs, separated

Soak the gelatin in the water. Combine the wine, sugar, and lemon juice, and zest in the top of a double boiler over hot water. When mixture is hot, add the dissolved gelatin and stir until all is dissolved. Beat the egg yolks until they are very thick and stir gradually into the lemon/gelatin mixture. Cook custard a few minutes, then remove from heat and cool.

Beat egg whites until stiff and gently fold into cooled lemon custard. Spoon the mousse into chilled 1½-quart bowl and refrigerate until it is firm, but still light, about 2–4 hours.
SERVES 4.

Soufflés

My Company Soufflé
Grand Marnier Soufflé
Pot de Crème Soufflé
Never-Miss Chocolate Soufflé
Versatile Chocolate Soufflé
Chocolate Roll Soufflé
Chestnut Soufflé
Skillet Soufflé
Frozen Chocolate Soufflé
"21" Club Frozen Soufflé
Frozen Lemon Soufflé
Soufflé Variations

My Company Soufflé

When I am entertaining royalty, or its equivalent, I make this soufflé because it's really elegant.

2½-quart soufflé dish, buttered and dusted with granulated sugar
3 tablespoons butter
3 tablespoons flour
1 cup milk
½ cup sugar
Pinch salt
6 egg yolks
2 squares bitter chocolate
¼ cup hot black coffee
1 teaspoon vanilla
1 tablespoon rum
8–10 ladyfingers or the equivalent in spongecake fingers
Cointreau or cognac
8 egg whites

FLUFFY SAUCE:
1¼ cups confectioners' sugar, sifted
8 tablespoons butter, softened
1 egg, separated
½ teaspoon vanilla
1 tablespoon rum
Pinch salt

Preheat oven to 375°F.

Melt the butter in a saucepan, blend in the flour, and gradually add the milk. Stir and cook until the mixture is thick, 3–5 minutes. Add sugar, salt, and well-beaten yolks. Divide this mixture into two equal parts. Flavor one part with chocolate melted down with coffee—taste for sweetness. Flavor the second part with vanilla and rum.

Soak ladyfingers in Cointreau or cognac until just soft.

Beat egg whites until firm, and fold half into each mixture.

Pour the chocolate mixture into the soufflé dish; arrange ladyfingers on this, and then top with vanilla-rum mixture. Bake 20–35 minutes. This is very spectacular.

In top of a double boiler, beat sugar into butter. Add yolk and flavorings, and place over hot water and heat until sauce is slightly thickened. Cool. Whip egg white with salt until stiff and fold into cooled sauce. Chill—then serve over My Company Soufflé.
SERVES 8–10.

Grand Marnier Soufflé

Grand Marnier is one of my favorite liqueurs and it does make a delicious soufflé.

2-quart soufflé dish, buttered and dusted with granulated sugar. Wrap the top of the soufflé dish with a band of foil or waxed paper, tied securely. Butter the inside of the collar.
8 egg yolks
⅔ cup sugar
½ cup Grand Marnier
10 egg whites
Pinch cream of tartar
Granulated sugar

Preheat oven to 450°F.

Place the yolks in the top of a double boiler and beat them until they are lemon colored. Gradually beat in the sugar. Cook this mixture over simmering water, stirring constantly. When mixture has thickened, remove from heat, and place over bowl of ice, and add the liqueur, stirring until blended. On a large flat platter, beat the egg whites with the cream of tartar until they peak. Transfer the yolk mixture to a very large bowl, and gently fold in the beaten whites until blended. Spoon batter into prepared soufflé dish and bake in preheated oven for 15 minutes. Sprinkle the top with sugar, remove collar, and serve at once.
SERVES 6.

Pot de Crème Soufflé

2-quart baking dish, buttered
6 eggs, separated
1 cup sugar
1 cup grated bitter chocolate

Preheat oven to 325°F.

Beat egg yolks and sugar until light and thick. Add chocolate. Fold in the stiffly beaten egg whites. Bake in a greased baking dish, set in pan of hot water in oven for about 1 hour, or until it is light and fluffy. Serve with cold cream, or whipped, sweetened cream.
SERVES 6–8.

Never-Miss Chocolate Soufflé

This soufflé will not fall. It can stand 30 minutes if not removed from the oven; just turn down the heat and leave the oven door open.

2-quart casserole
1 square bitter chocolate
2 heaping tablespoons cocoa
1 tablespoon flour or
    cornstarch
1 cup sugar
4 eggs, separated
1½ cups milk
2 tablespoons butter
1 tablespoon vanilla

Preheat oven to 325°F.

Combine chocolate, cocoa, flour or cornstarch, and sugar. Blend into well-beaten yolks. Mix in milk and butter and cook in a double boiler over boiling water until thick, stirring constantly. Add vanilla and beat as it cools.

When cool, beat egg whites until stiff and fold into mixture, pour into casserole, and set in pan of warm water. Bake in oven for 1 hour—or until knife inserted in center comes out clean. Serve at once with sweetened whipped cream, plain cream, or chocolate sauce.
SERVES 6.

Versatile Chocolate Soufflé

The French have a way with soufflés—this is light and delightful to eat. It is also the base for the next recipe, Chocolate Roll Soufflé (p. 138).

1-quart soufflé dish, buttered
6 eggs, separated
¾ cup sugar
Pinch salt
6 ounces semisweet chocolate
Few drops hot black coffee
1 teaspoon vanilla
Whipped cream

Preheat oven to 375°F.

Beat egg yolks until stiff and lemony. Gradually add sugar and salt. Melt chocolate with a few drops of hot coffee, stir in the vanilla, and combine with yolks and sugar. Beat whites until stiff and fold a quarter of whites thoroughly into yolk mixture, then add rest of whites, folding gently. Pour into soufflé dish and bake about 20 minutes or until it rises and is light and puffy. Serve with whipped cream.
SERVES 6–8.

Chocolate Roll Soufflé

15" × 10" × 1" pan, line
  with waxed paper, then
  butter paper
Versatile Chocolate Soufflé
  (see p. 137)
Confectioners' sugar
Cocoa
1 cup heavy cream
1 tablespoon sugar

Preheat oven to 350°F.

Prepare soufflé mixture as in Versatile Chocolate Soufflé recipe. Pour soufflé mixture into pan and bake for 15–20 minutes. Remove from oven and top with a damp towel. Sprinkle another towel, waxed paper, or foil with confectioners' sugar and cocoa. Turn the pan over to turn the soufflé out upside down on the paper, and remove the waxed paper in which it was cooked. Let it cool slightly. Whip the cream with the sugar, then spread over soufflé and roll up gently, jelly-roll fashion, using the paper under it to ease it over. When cool, serve, cut into slices.
SERVES 6–8.

Chestnut Soufflé

Long ago as a housewife living in Dallas, I kept a charge account at Bloomingdale's just to order Maillard's chocolate and Faugier's canned chestnuts. For chocolate chestnut lovers, this is it!

1½-quart mold, buttered and
  dusted with granulated
  sugar
2 tablespoons butter
2 tablespoons all-purpose
  flour
1 cup chestnut purée, un-
  sweetened
1 cup milk
½ cup sugar
2½ ounces bitter chocolate,
  melted
4 eggs, separated
1¼ teaspoons vanilla

Preheat oven to 375°F.

In a saucepan melt the butter and mix in the flour. In an electric mixer, blend the chestnut purée with the milk and sugar, then add to the butter mixture slowly. Stir this over low heat until thickened. Add the melted chocolate and blend. Beat yolks and slowly add to the purée, blend well, and cool. When thoroughly cooled, add vanilla and stiffly beaten egg whites. Spoon into prepared mold, place in pan of hot water, and bake 40–45 minutes. Serve immediately.
SERVES 8.

Skillet Soufflé

Use a cast-iron skillet for this soufflé. For a novice this is almost foolproof.

10" cast-iron skillet, buttered
 and dusted with granulated
 sugar
8 eggs, separated
¾ cup sugar
⅓ cup rum or cognac—the
 French prefer cognac
Granulated sugar
½ cup extra rum or cognac

Preheat oven to 375°F.

Beat the yolks until light and fluffy. Slowly add the sugar and beat until blended, then add the rum or cognac. Beat egg whites until they hold a peak. Fold them gently but thoroughly into the yolk mixture. Heat the prepared skillet, then spoon in the soufflé mixture and bake about 15 minutes. Remove from the oven, dust with granulated sugar, sprinkle extra rum or cognac over the top, ignite, and serve from skillet. Serve immediately.

SERVES 8.

VARIATION:
Substitute either ½ cup orange juice with zest of the orange or ¼ cup lemon juice and matching zest. For either, cognac may be used to flambé, or Cointreau for a fruitier flavor. You may even blend the two fruits.

Frozen Chocolate Soufflé

This is one of the most glamorous dessert soufflés in my repertoire.

1½-quart soufflé mold, lightly
 buttered
1½ cups granulated sugar
⅔ cup strong coffee
4 egg yolks
6 ounces semisweet chocolate,
 melted
1 pint whipping cream,
 whipped
Lightly sweetened whipped
 cream
Shaved bitter chocolate

Combine sugar and half the coffee in saucepan and boil until it spins a thread or registers 240° on candy thermometer. Beat the egg yolks thoroughly in an electric mixer and gradually pour the hot syrup over the yolks, beating constantly. Melt chocolate in saucepan with remaining coffee and beat into yolk mixture. Continue to beat until cool.

Fold in the whipped cream and pour into prepared soufflé dish. Cover tightly with foil and freeze 3–4 hours. Remove the foil, invert on cold platter and serve with additional lightly sweetened whipped cream and shaved bitter chocolate.

SERVES 6–8.

"21" Club Frozen Soufflé

This is purported to be their recipe. Even if it isn't, it's great, and easy to make.

3-cup mold
1 pint vanilla ice cream, softened
3 almond macaroons, crumbled
1½ tablespoons Grand Marnier or the great Italian Aurum
½ cup heavy cream, whipped
3 tablespoons sliced toasted almonds
2 teaspoons confectioners' sugar

To softened ice cream add crumbled macaroons, liqueur, and whipped cream. Spoon into 3-cup mold. Sprinkle with toasted almonds and confectioners' sugar. Cover with foil and freeze 4–5 hours. When ready to serve, unmold and serve with berry sauce.

BERRY SAUCE:
Fresh berries are always preferable, but if unavailable use the frozen.

1 pint fresh strawberries, halved or 1 10-ounce package sliced, frozen strawberries, thawed
4 tablespoons sugar for fresh berries or 2 tablespoons for frozen
1½ tablespoons Grand Marnier or Aurum

Put berries in saucepan with the sugar, and simmer until soft but not mushy. Add the liqueur and serve.
SERVES 4.

Frozen Lemon Soufflé

This is strictly for lemon-lovers, and it will bring raves! Use a mold that is pretty enough to be brought to the table.

6-cup mold
12 egg yolks
1¾ cups sugar
½ cup fresh lemon juice,
  unstrained
¼ cup fresh orange juice,
  unstrained
1 tablespoon lemon zest
1 tablespoon orange zest
6 egg whites
⅛ teaspoon salt
¾ cup heavy cream, whipped
Lightly sweetened whipped
  cream
Fresh raspberries or strawberries

Combine yolks with sugar in top of double boiler and beat until light. Add juices and zest. Then place top of double boiler over rapidly boiling water and continue to beat until thick and creamy. Remove from heat and cool completely.

Beat egg whites until stiff with the salt. Fold gently into the cooled lemon mixture.

Beat heavy cream until stiff and fold into the lemon soufflé, blending carefully. Spoon into the mold and freeze.

To serve, pass a bowl of lightly sweetened whipped cream and fresh raspberries or straw-berries.
SERVES 8–10

VARIATION:
Toasted freshly grated coconut may be sprinkled over the top before serving.

Soufflé Variations

Soak 1 cup candied, chopped fruit in cognac, and add to egg yolk mixture. Flavor with 1 teaspoon vanilla.

Soak 2 cups almond macaroons in ½ cup Cointreau or cognac and spoon into soufflé dish alternately with soufflé mixture, always ending with soufflé mix on top.

Omit the vanilla. Add to the yolk mixture, before folding in the beaten whites 1½ tablespoons orange zest, 1½ teaspoons grated lemon zest, and 6 tablespoons Grand Marnier. Sprinkle the top of the soufflé with granulated sugar about 4–5 minutes before it is done. This will crystalize the top.

Crème de la Crème

Lemon Meringue Pudding
Cocoa Fudge-Top Pudding
Marquise au Chocolat
Crème Caramel
Birdie's Cabinet Pudding
Old-Fashioned Rice Pudding
Chocolate Sabayon
Pot de Crème
Light Pot de Crème
Chestnut Pot de Crème
Spanish Cream
Crème Duchesse
Crème Brulée
Crème Caramel au Chocolat
Chestnut Bombe
Chocolate Bavarian Cream
Hershey Freeze
Amy Vanderbilt's Frozen Cream
Harriet Rose's Prune Cream
Tipsy Frozen Parfait
Russian Cream
Tillie's Charlotte Russe
Prune Mallow
Frozen Lemon Dessert
Apricot Cream Mold
Chocolate Icebox Cake I
Chocolate Icebox Cake II
Ladyfinger Supreme

Lemon Meringue Pudding

A lovely ending to a summer dinner.

8" glass baking dish, buttered
2 tablespoons butter
1 cup sugar
3½ tablespoons flour
6 tablespoons lemon juice
3 eggs, separated, at room
   temperature
Grated zest of 1 lemon
1¼ cups milk
Pinch salt
1 cup strawberries, washed,
   dried, and stemmed, then
   lightly crushed
1 cup heavy cream

Preheat oven to 350°F.

In a bowl, cream the butter with ⅔ cup sugar, then add the flour and lemon juice. Blend well. Beat the egg yolks until light and add the zest of lemon and the milk. Combine with butter and sugar mixture. Beat egg whites with salt and remaining ⅓ cup sugar until stiff but not dry. Fold into yolk mixture gently. Spoon batter into prepared baking dish, set in pan of hot water, and bake in preheated oven for about 1 hour. Remove from oven, let cool, then chill thoroughly. Serve with crushed strawberries and pass a pitcher of cold heavy cream.
SERVES 6–8.

Cocoa Fudge-Top Pudding

I like the brownie-like consistency of this pudding.

8" × 8" × 2" pan, buttered
⅔ cups all-purpose flour,
   sifted
½ teaspoon baking powder
¼ teaspoon salt
10 tablespoons cocoa
⅔ cup chopped walnuts or
   pecans
10–11 tablespoons soft butter
1 cup granulated sugar
2 eggs
1 teaspoon vanilla
1 cup brown sugar, packed
2 cups hot water

Preheat oven to 350°F.

Sift flour, baking powder, salt, and 4 tablespoons cocoa into a bowl. Add nuts and mix. In an electric mixer, combine butter and granulated sugar, and beat until creamy. Add eggs and vanilla, and beat until smooth. Stir in the dry ingredients and blend. Spoon the batter into prepared pan.

Combine the brown sugar, remaining 6 tablespoons of cocoa, and hot water in a bowl. Beat well, then pour evenly over the batter in the pan. Bake about 50 minutes. Serve warm.
SERVES 8–10.

Marquise au Chocolat

This is truly an exquisite French dessert. It is easy to prepare, just takes a little time—about one hour—and patience.

2–2½-quart mold
½ cup sugar
½ cup milk
⅛ teaspoon vanilla
3 egg yolks, beaten
3 sticks sweet butter
¼ pound bittersweet chocolate
2 tablespoons water

In the top of a double boiler dissolve the sugar and milk with the vanilla. Bring the mixture to a boil, then let it cool. Slowly add the beaten egg yolks. Place top of double boiler over slowly simmering water and stir it constantly until thickened. Remove from heat and cool.

In an electric mixer, cream the butter until very soft—on medium to slow speed.

Melt the chocolate with the water over low heat, cool, then slowly add it to the creamed butter. Blend, then add the cooled custard and slowly beat the mixture on low speed for 20 minutes. Pour the finished custard into the mold and chill it for several hours. Unmold, slice, and serve to each guest with this sauce:

SAUCE:
2 cups milk
3 tablespoons sugar
⅛ teaspoon vanilla
6 egg yolks, beaten

In the top of a double boiler, combine milk, sugar, and vanilla. Bring to a boil to dissolve the sugar. Cool the milk a little, then slowly stir it into the beaten egg yolks. Return to double boiler and stir over simmering water until sauce is thickened. Chill the sauce and serve it cold.
SERVES 6–8.

Crème Caramel

This custard is a favorite on almost every menu across Europe. In Portugal, orange zest and juice is added for flavor. I am a purist and prefer it as it is presented here.

2½-quart glass baking dish
½ cup sugar plus 4 table-
    spoons
½ cup boiling water
2 eggs
3 egg yolks
Pinch salt
1 teaspoon vanilla
1½ cups hot milk

Preheat oven to 250°F.

Melt ½ cup sugar in a heavy saucepan, stirring constantly, until it browns. Very slowly add the ½ cup of boiling water, stirring to keep it from boiling over. Reduce heat and simmer the caramel for 3–4 minutes, then pour it into the baking dish, turning and tilting the dish to coat the entire inside surface.

With a wire wisk, beat the eggs and yolks with the salt, 4 tablespoons sugar, and vanilla. When this is well blended, slowly stir in the hot milk and mix. Pour this custard into the caramel-lined baking dish and set in a shallow pan of hot water. Bake in preheated oven for 1 hour. When a knife inserted in the center comes out clean, it is done. Chill for several hours, then invert onto serving plate. The caramel will adhere and cover the custard like a sauce. This may be sliced and served.

SERVES 6.

Birdie's Cabinet Pudding

Mrs. Albert Linz, Aunt Birdie, was a lady who entertained lavishly and set a marvelous table. This was one of her favorite desserts.

8-cup mold
6 tablespoons sugar
5 egg yolks
1½ envelopes plain gelatin
½ cup cold water
¾ cup bourbon whiskey
¾ cup chopped almonds
1 small bottle maraschino
  cherries, drained
12 almond macaroons,
  crumbed
3 egg whites, beaten to stiff
  peak
2 cups heavy cream, whipped
Sweetened whipped cream
Drained stemmed cherries
Almond slivers

Combine sugar and egg yolks in top of double boiler and cook over simmering water a few minutes until sugar is dissolved and mixture blended. Remove from heat. Soak gelatin in ½ cup cold water and add to hot egg mixture. Stir till gelatin dissolves. Add the whiskey, almonds, drained cherries, and macaroon crumbs. Cool. Fold in the beaten egg whites and the whipped heavy cream. Pour into mold and chill 4–5 hours. Unmold and serve with additional sweetened whipped cream and decorated with drained stemmed cherries and toasted almond slivers. SERVES 8.

Old-Fashioned Rice Pudding

My foreman, Howard Bauer, graciously gave me this recipe, his grand-mother's. The pudding cuts like a cake. Serve it warm with raspberry jam or cold with sliced fresh fruit.

9" × 11" pan, buttered
2 cups water
1 teaspoon salt
1 cup uncooked rice
½ cup plus 2 tablespoons
  sugar
3 eggs
1½ teaspoons vanilla
2 cups milk
1 cup Sultana raisins
1 teaspoon cinnamon
Butter

Preheat oven to 350°F.
    Combine water and salt and bring to a boil, add rice and cook until soft. Drain and rinse immediately with cold water.
    While rice is cooking, combine ½ cup sugar, eggs, and vanilla in large bowl and blend well. Add the milk, mix and add the cooked rice and raisins. Spoon into prepared baking dish.
    Blend together the 2 tablespoons sugar and cinnamon and sprinkle over pudding. Dot with butter and bake in preheated oven for 45 minutes.
SERVES 10–12.

Chocolate Sabayon

A lovely holiday dessert, especially for buffet dinners.

8 eggs, separated
1 cup confectioners' sugar
½ cup Madeira wine
2 ounces dark, sweet chocolate, grated
Pinch salt
2 cups heavy cream
2 tablespoons granulated sugar

Place the egg yolks and confectioners' sugar in top of double boiler over boiling water, and beat with an egg beater or whisk until frothy. Add the wine and continue to beat the mixture until thick and doubled. Remove it from the heat and add the grated chocolate. Continue to stir until chocolate is melted. Cool.

Whip egg whites until stiff with pinch of salt. Whip the heavy cream with the granulated sugar. Fold the beaten whites and whipped cream into the cooled custard and spoon into sherbet or parfait glasses. Chill thoroughly, at least 2–3 hours.

SERVES 8–10.

VARIATION:
Here are some suggestions to add to this recipe. If you add them all, the dessert will serve at least four more persons. The fruit and nuts are added just before the egg whites and whipped cream.

¼ cup diced candied cherries
½ cup diced candied pineapple
½ cup chopped pecans

Garnish with bits of candied cherries. Either variation may be frozen in freezer trays and served in cut squares. Be sure to cover with foil.

Pot de Crème

You really can't be calorie-conscious and enjoy this! I have a favorite cousin who insists his portion be served in a large Irish coffee cup instead of the usual pot de crème or demitasse cups.

2 cups milk
1 pound Maillard's sweet
   chocolate (double eagle)
6 egg yolks, very well-beaten

In a saucepan, scald the milk, add the chocolate, and cook over moderate heat, stirring constantly, until chocolate is melted and mixture reaches just to the boiling point. Pour this slowly and carefully over the beaten egg yolks and stir until blended. Strain through a fine sieve into small cups and chill. Serve very cold.
SERVES 8.

Light Pot de Crème

This is so named as it is lighter in color and less rich than the usual pot de crème, owing to the fact that half the amount of chocolate is required. It is a delicious dessert, but never to be compared with the real Pot de Crème.

1 pint of milk
½ pound dark sweet chocolate
6 egg yolks

Combine the milk and chocolate in top of double boiler over simmering water, stirring frequently, until chocolate is completely melted and milk is scalded. Remove from heat. Beat yolks until light and lemony and slowly add the yolks to the chocolate. When well blended, strain this through a fine strainer into pot de crème cups, demitasse cups, or glasses. Chill several hours before serving. This may be served with an extra topping of sweetened, whipped cream.
SERVES 6–8.

Chestnut Pot de Crème

This is not a real pot de crème, but it is very rich and I serve it in my demitasse cups or the tiny pots.

1 small can sweetened
    chestnuts, puréed (6¾
    ounces)
1 cup heavy cream, whipped
1 teaspoon vanilla

Blend all and spoon into the cups. Chill 2–3 hours.
SERVES 6.

Spanish Cream

An easy dessert that can be prepared ahead of time.

6 individual dessert dishes or
    ramekins
1 envelope unflavored gelatin
6 tablespoons sugar, divided
⅛ teaspoon salt
2 eggs, separated
2 cups milk, divided
1¼ teaspoons vanilla
6 whole strawberries, washed
    and stemmed

Combine the gelatin, 2 tablespoons of the sugar, and the salt in a saucepan. Beat together the egg yolks and 1 cup of the milk and add to the gelatin mixture. Place over very low heat, stirring constantly, until the gelatin is dissolved, about 5 minutes. Remove from the heat, add remaining 1 cup of milk and vanilla, and blend well. Chill until the mixture mounds slightly when dropped from a spoon.

Beat the egg whites until stiff but not dry. Gradually add remaining 4 tablespoons of sugar and beat until very stiff. Fold into gelatin mixture and spoon into individual serving dishes. Chill until firm.

SAUCE:
1 6-ounce package semisweet
    chocolate bits
¾ cup water
Pinch salt

Combine all in top of double boiler and melt over hot water. Store in refrigerator until ready to use.

Garnish each serving with a strawberry and pass a chocolate sauce for the topping.
SERVES 6.

Crème Duchesse

This is a creamless mousse, but it is one of the richest desserts imaginable—and well worth every calorie!

6-cup ring mold, buttered
8 ounces dark sweet chocolate
4 eggs, separated
½ cup sugar
1 stick butter, softened
1 cup heavy cream, whipped
1–2 tablespoons brandy
1 tablespoon confectioners'
  sugar

Melt the chocolate in the top of a double boiler over hot (not boiling) water; cool. Beat the egg yolks until frothy, add the sugar, and continue beating until thick and lemon-colored. Add the cooled chocolate and beat again; add the softened butter and beat until the mixture is thick and creamy.

Whip the egg whites until stiff and fold in gently. Pour into prepared ring mold and chill until set, about 3–4 hours.

Whip cream with brandy and confectioners' sugar. To serve, turn out on chilled plate and fill the center with the flavored whipped cream. SERVES 6–8.

Crème Brulée

I am a purist at heart, and I prepare this crème when I am in a romantic mood and for very special people—my family! There are many variations on the theme that will be listed below—but do try it my way first. The beauty of this marvelous dessert is that it can be prepared a day ahead, then finished with the topping before serving.

The perfect topping is a bowl of fresh raspberries passed along with the dessert. To serve you will need a heavy spoon to crack the top!

3-quart glass baking dish,
  buttered lightly
4 cups heavy cream
8 egg yolks
Dark brown sugar
Fresh raspberries

Heat the cream in the top of a double boiler, let it come to a boil, and boil for one minute. Remove from the heat. Beat the egg yolks and pour in a thin stream into the cream, beating constantly. Return to the double boiler and cook over low heat for about 5 minutes, never letting it boil, but just to the boiling point. Pour into prepared glass baking dish and chill in the refrigerator, uncovered. The custard will set.

Before serving, sift the brown sugar over the top of the crème, using a coarse textured sifter. Make an even layer ¼" thick. Place custard under a broiler at least 6" from the flame, leaving the door open, until a crust of caramelized sugar is formed. This only takes a few seconds. Serve immediately or refrigerate until serving time. I prefer to chill it again.
SERVES 8–10.

VARIATION:
After beating in egg yolks, add to crème 6 tablespoons sugar and 2 teaspoons vanilla, or omit the vanilla and add 2 tablespoons brandy, rum, or orange liqueur.

Crème Caramel au Chocolat

No matter where you travel in Europe, the standard dessert in all countries is crème caramel. This is a welcome variation on the old theme if you are a chocolate addict.

8 small custard molds
1 cup sugar, divided
2 tablespoons water
Juice of ½ lemon
2 cups milk
4½ squares semisweet chocolate
4 eggs
4 egg yolks

Preheat oven to 350°F.

In a small saucepan, bring ½ cup sugar, water, and lemon juice to a boil, and cook until the syrup becomes a dark amber. Divide equally among the 8 custard cups. Cool. In a small saucepan, combine the milk with the chocolate, stirring constantly until melted. Beat eggs, yolks, and ½ cup sugar until smooth and thickened. Combine with the milk mixture and blend well. Strain through a fine strainer into the custard cups. Place cups in pan and pour boiling water around them. Place in oven and bake about 30 minutes. Custards should be set. Remove from oven, let cool, then refrigerate. Unmold and serve.
SERVES 8.

Chestnut Bombe

Chestnuts lend a gourmet touch and quality to many desserts. Here is another for your collection.

2-quart mold
1 quart rich vanilla ice cream,
    softened to spread
2 egg whites
½ cup sugar
¼ cup water
1 teaspoon gelatin, un-
    flavored, dissolved in 1½
    tablespoons hot water
1½ cups canned sweet
    chestnuts, chopped
2 teaspoons vanilla
2 cups heavy cream, whipped

Spread softened ice cream in mold and freeze. Beat egg whites until stiff. Cook sugar and water for about 5 minutes, to the thread stage, and slowly pour over egg whites in thin steady stream, beating whites all the while. Add dissolved gelatin to egg white mixture. Set all over a bowl of cracked ice and stir until cold. Add chopped chestnuts and vanilla, then fold in the whipped cream. Spoon over frozen vanilla ice cream and freeze again. Unmold to serve or serve from mold.
SERVES 8–10.

Chocolate Bavarian Cream

Most Bavarian creams that are listed in today's cookbooks call for gelatin as the base for molding. This one is typically French as it calls for just a touch of flour for the custard.

8 custard cups
1 cup milk, divided
1 teaspoon flour
4 eggs, separated
3 tablespoons sugar
4 ounces semisweet chocolate
½ cup heavy cream, whipped
1 teaspoon vanilla

Blend 2 tablespoons milk with the flour and set aside. Beat the egg yolks until they are thick and lemony. Add the flour mixture and the sugar. Blend well.

Melt the chocolate with the remaining milk in the top of a double boiler over hot water, stirring until blended. Remove from heat and cool. Combine with the egg mixture and return to top of double boiler, still over the hot water, and cook, stirring constantly, until custard thickens. Remove from heat, pour into a chilled bowl, and let cool.

Beat egg whites until stiff, fold in the whipped cream and vanilla, and then gently fold into the

chocolate custard, blending well. Spoon into 8 custard cups and chill for at least 6 hours or overnight.
SERVES 8.

Hershey Freeze

A great last-minute dessert.

4-cup mold, lightly buttered
1⅓ cups Hershey chocolate
 syrup
2 cups heavy cream, whipped
3½ tablespoons curaçao,
 Grand Marnier, or rum
Chopped walnuts, pecans, or
 toasted almonds
Bitter chocolate for shaving

Fold the syrup into the whipped cream; add the liqueur and freeze in mold for 2–3 hours. Garnish with the chopped nuts and shaved bitter chocolate.
SERVES 6–8.

Amy Vanderbilt's Frozen Cream

Miss Vanderbilt was a very good business friend of mine. More than that, she was a noted hostess for dessert parties. This was one of her favorites.

½ pound almond brittle,
 crushed
2 cups heavy cream, whipped
2 tablespoons Amaretto

Combine all, pour into pot de crème or demitasse cups and freeze 1 hour.
SERVES 6–8.

Harriet Rose's Prune Cream

My dear friend Harriet is a fabulous hostess and a perfectionist in the kitchen. Be sure to try this.

1½-quart mold, dipped in cool
    water and shaken out
1 tablespoon unflavored
    gelatin
1 tablespoon cold water
1 cup hot prune purée (1½
    jars junior baby food)
¾ cup sugar
¼ cup bourbon
½ teaspoon lemon juice
1½ cups heavy cream,
    whipped
Candied chestnuts
Lightly sweetened whipped
    cream

Soak the gelatin in the cold water in a double boiler over hot water. Stir dissolved gelatin into hot prune purée. Add sugar and cool. Stir in the bourbon and lemon juice. When mixture thickens add the whipped cream and spoon into wet mold and chill. Serve with additional lightly sweetened whipped cream and decorate with candied chestnuts.
SERVES 8.

VARIATION:
Blend some nesselrode into the whipped cream topping.

Tipsy Frozen Parfait

A lovely do-ahead dessert for a crowd.

3 quarts vanilla ice cream,
    softened
½ cup bourbon
3 tablespoons light rum
1 cup heavy cream, whipped
18–20 almond macaroons,
    crumbled (reserve ½ cup)
1 cup crushed pineapple,
    drained
¾ cup maraschino cherries,
    halved
2 cups chopped toasted
    walnuts

Blend ice cream well with liquors, gently fold in the whipped cream, cookie crumbs, fruit, and nuts. Spoon into 18–20 parfait glasses, garnish with reserved crumbs and freeze at least 2 hours.
SERVES 18–20.

Russian Cream

This is simple and simply delicious.

1½-quart mold, dipped into cool water and shaken out
1 tablespoon gelatin
½ cup cold water
1 cup light cream
¾ cup sugar
1 cup sour cream
½ teaspoon vanilla
¼ teaspoon salt
Fresh red raspberries

Soak the gelatin in cold water for about 5 minutes. Combine the light cream and sugar in top of double boiler and place over hot water until warm and sugar is dissolved. Remove from heat and add gelatin. Chill. When slightly thickened, beat until stiff, then fold in the sour cream slightly beaten with vanilla and salt. Pour into wet mold and chill. Unmold and serve with raspberries.
SERVES 6.

Tillie's Charlotte Russe

Tillie Metzler was an institution in Dallas. She enjoyed being a caterer during the twenties and thirties when ladies were not aware of calories and waistlines!

8" springform, buttered
24 large marshmallows
⅔ cup milk
3 tablespoons rum or whiskey—more if desired
2 cups heavy cream, whipped
18 plain ladyfingers, split

Melt marshmallows with the milk in the top of a double boiler, then cool. Add the rum and whipped cream. Line bottom and sides of the springform with the ladyfingers. (Be sure the cut side of ladyfinger faces inward.) Pour mixture into form and refrigerate overnight. Decorate with bittersweet chocolate curls, toasted almonds, or fresh strawberries.
SERVES 8.

Prune Mallow

Little kids and big kids like this, and it is easy!

20 large marshmallows
2½ tablespoons water
2 tablespoons lemon juice
1 5-ounce jar puréed
  prunes—Gerbers or Heinz
1 cup heavy cream, whipped

In the top of a double boiler over simmering water, dissolve the marshmallows in the water and the lemon juice. Add the puréed prunes. Remove from heat and cool thoroughly. Blend the whipped cream into the mixture and chill or freeze.
SERVES 6–8.

Frozen Lemon Dessert

The return for the small effort is worth it. Strawberries add a festive look.

10" × 6" × 1½" glass bak-
  ing dish, buttered
24 vanilla wafers, crushed
3 eggs, separated
½ cup sugar plus ⅓ cup
⅛ teaspoon salt
1½ teaspoons grated lemon
  zest
3 tablespoons lemon juice
1 cup heavy cream, whipped

Press the vanilla wafer crumbs in an even layer into the bottom and sides of the buttered baking dish. Beat the egg yolks in the top of a double boiler over simmering water until thick and lemony. Slowly add the ½ cup sugar, salt, zest, and lemon juice, and cook over simmering water until thick, stirring constantly. Cool to room temperature.

Beat the egg whites to soft peaks and slowly add the ⅓ cup sugar, beating until stiff. Fold into the lemon mixture gently, then fold the whipped cream into the custard and blend. Pour into prepared dish and freeze until firm, 2–3 hours. Cut into squares.
SERVES 12–14.

Apricot Cream Mold

A good summer or winter dessert.

1-quart mold
1 cup dried apricots
2 teaspoons fresh lemon juice
1 teaspoon lemon zest
2 egg yolks, beaten
1 cup confectioners' sugar, sifted
½ teaspoon vanilla
Pinch salt
1 cup heavy cream, whipped
½ cup toasted sliced almonds

Place apricots in saucepan with water to cover and cook until tender. Drain and, while still hot, purée with lemon juice and zest. Cool.

Combine beaten yolks with confectioners' sugar, vanilla, and salt and continue to beat until thick and creamy.

Fold apricot purée into whipped cream; fold in yolk mixture. Spoon into mold and chill for 3–4 hours. Unmold and garnish with toasted almonds.
SERVES 8.

Chocolate Icebox Cake I

My mother-in-law was almost helpless in the kitchen. However, this was one of her specialties and a favorite of the family.

9" × 4" × 2" loaf pan, buttered bottom and sides
2 dozen plain ladyfingers
2 sticks sweet butter
1 cup confectioners' sugar
2 ounces bitter chocolate
¼ cup water
½ cup granulated sugar
4 eggs, separated
Lightly sweetened whipped cream
Shaved bittersweet chocolate

Split the ladyfingers and line the bottom and sides of the buttered pan with them, cut side facing inward.

Cream the butter with the confectioners' sugar. Combine chocolate, water, and granulated sugar in top of double boiler over simmering water and blend well until chocolate is melted. Beat egg yolks and slowly add to chocolate mixture. Cook until smooth, stirring constantly. Remove from heat and cool completely.

Beat egg whites to stiff peaks and fold into chocolate mixture, blending gently but thoroughly. Pour into prepared pan and refrigerate overnight. Unmold to serve, top with lightly sweetened whipped cream and shaved bittersweet chocolate.
SERVES 8.

Chocolate Icebox Cake II

In parting with this recipe, I am divulging an old family treasure. My father insisted that it had to be chocolate to be dessert. I still feel that way today, and so does my family.

9" × 5" × 2¾" loaf pan,
    lightly buttered
2 sticks butter
½ cup granulated sugar
1 cup confectioners' sugar
2 ounces bitter chocolate
¼ cup strong coffee
4 eggs, separated
30 plain ladyfingers, split
1 cup heavy cream
1 tablespoon confectioners'
    sugar
1 teaspoon vanilla
Shaved bitter chocolate for
    garnish

In an electric mixer, cream the butter and granulated sugar until light and fluffy. Combine confectioners' sugar, chocolate, and coffee in top of double boiler and cook over simmering water, stirring frequently, until chocolate is melted.

Beat egg yolks until light, then with chocolate removed from heat, combine yolks and chocolate; return to heat and cook, stirring constantly, until thick and smooth. Add to the butter mixture and blend thoroughly. Cool. Beat egg whites until stiff and gently fold into the mixture.

Line the bottom and sides of the loaf pan with split ladyfingers, arranging them cut side in and touching each other. Pour in half of the chocolate mixture. Add a layer of ladyfingers laid crosswise. Pour in the remaining chocolate and add another layer of ladyfingers. Cover with waxed paper and chill 4–5 hours. Unmold on a chilled serving plate. Frost top and sides of the cake with the heavy cream that has been whipped with the 1 tablespoon of confectioners' sugar and 1 teaspoon vanilla. Sprinkle with shaved bitter chocolate if desired.
SERVES 8.

Ladyfinger Supreme

When I was a bride, my husband laid down a very strict rule for dessert—"Don't serve me any dessert made with lemons!" I didn't, but my family had a more varied palate, so he always had a separate goodie. Many years later, when his tastes had changed and he had mellowed, he tasted this divine creation and it became his favorite.

9" × 4" × 2½" loaf pan, buttered bottom and sides
2 packages plain ladyfingers, split
1 cup sugar
1 cup butter
3 eggs, separated
Juice of 1½ large oranges (do not strain)
Grated zest of the oranges
Juice of 1 large lemon (do not strain)
Grated zest of the lemon
Lightly sweetened whipped cream
Fresh strawberries, whole or sliced

Line bottom and sides of loaf pan with ladyfingers, split side facing inward.

Combine the sugar and butter and beat until light and creamy. Add the egg yolks, one at a time, blend well, then add the fruit juices and zests. Beat the egg whites until stiff and gently fold into the mixture. Spoon a layer on ladyfingers, cover with another layer of ladyfingers, repeat until all layers are complete with ladyfingers on top. Cover with plastic wrap or foil and freeze. To serve, unmold and spread top with lightly sweetened whipped cream. Stud the top with whole or sliced fresh strawberries.
SERVES 8.

Ice Creams

Chocolate Maple Ice Cream
French Chocolate Ice Cream
Rum Chocolate Macaroon Ice Cream
Mocha-Chocolate Chip Ice Cream
Kahlua Freeze
Chocolate Custard Ice Cream
Coffee Liqueur Ice Cream
Peach or Strawberry Ice Cream
Strawberry Gin Ice Cream
Pineapple Pistachio Ice Cream
Strawberry Sherbet
Raspberry Sherry Mold
Italian Cassata

Chocolate Maple Ice Cream

I think the walnuts add a delightful touch.

¼ pound caramels—half maple flavor, half chocolate
3 cups heavy cream
2 eggs
1 cup sugar
½ teaspoon vanilla
¼ cup chopped walnuts (optional)

Melt caramels with a little of the cream in the top of double boiler over low heat.

Beat eggs until light, and add sugar, continuing to beat. Add egg mixture to the candy mixture slowly, stirring constantly. Cool. Fold in the lightly beaten, not stiff, cream and vanilla, and pour into electric ice cream freezer. Freeze in the usual manner. If you want to add walnuts, fold them in with the cream.
MAKES 1½ QUARTS.

French Chocolate Ice Cream

2½ ounces bitter chocolate
2 cups milk
1¼ cups sugar
Pinch salt
1¾ teaspoons vanilla
2 cups heavy cream

Combine chocolate and milk in top of double boiler and cook over simmering water until the chocolate has dissolved. Stirring, add the sugar and salt. When sugar is dissolved, remove from heat and beat with whisk until frothy and cool. Add vanilla and stiffly whipped cream. Blend well, pour into electric freezer, and freeze in the usual manner.
MAKES 2 QUARTS.

Rum Chocolate Macaroon Ice Cream

Almost like a biscuit tortoni, only better!

1 dozen dry almond macaroons, crumbled
2 cups light or coffee cream
2 ounces bitter chocolate
1 cup granulated sugar
¼ cup hot water
1–2 tablespoons rum, or more, to taste
2 cups heavy cream

Mix crumbs with 1 cup coffee cream. Combine chocolate, sugar, and water in a saucepan and stir over low heat until melted. Cool and add to the crumb mixture with the rum and rest of creams. Pour into electric ice cream freezer and freeze according to the manufacturer's instructions.
MAKES 1½ QUARTS.

Mocha-Chocolate Chip Ice Cream

This pleases little kids and big kids alike!

3 eggs
¾ cup granulated sugar
½ teaspoon salt
½ cup milk
1 cup extra-strong black coffee
2 squares bitter chocolate, melted
1 tablespoon vanilla
3 cups light cream
¾ cup semisweet chocolate bits

Beat eggs, sugar, and salt until light. Scald the milk with the coffee and slowly add to the egg mixture. Transfer all to the top of a double boiler and cook over hot water, stirring constantly, until mixture becomes thick. Add melted chocolate. Remove from heat and cool. When cool, add the vanilla and cream. Mix in the chocolate bits and spoon into electric freezer and freeze according to manufacturer's directions.
MAKES 2 QUARTS.

Kahlua Freeze

I am partial to the combination of coffee and chocolate—and I think you will be, too.

1 cup heavy cream, whipped
2–3 tablespoons Kahlua, or more, to taste
1 pint chocolate or chocolate chocolate chip ice cream, softened

Combine all three, then freeze for at least 2 hours. Serve with an extra splash of Kahlua.
MAKES 1 QUART.

Chocolate Custard Ice Cream

An extra-creamy ice cream. Top each serving with a splash of Kahlua—a lovely touch!

2 cups granulated sugar
4 cups light or coffee cream
3 eggs
4 squares bitter chocolate, melted
2 teaspoons vanilla
4 cups heavy cream

Combine 1 cup of sugar with the cream in the top of a double boiler and scald.

In a bowl, combine the other cup of sugar with the eggs and beat until lemony, then very slowly add the scalded cream to the egg mixture, stirring constantly. When blended, add the melted chocolate and transfer all to the top of a double boiler. Cook over boiling water, stirring constantly, until thickened. Remove from heat and when cool, add vanilla and heavy cream. Pour into ice cream freezer and freeze according to manufacturer's instructions.
MAKES 2½ QUARTS.

Coffee Liqueur Ice Cream

If you are not a coffee addict, this will convert you!

4 cups heavy cream
2 cups light cream
1 cup sugar
¼ cup Kahlua or Tia Maria
4 tablespoons instant coffee
Pinch salt
Toasted almonds for garnish

Combine all ingredients except almonds and when well blended, pour into electric freezer and follow manufacturer's instructions. Serve the ice cream topped with toasted almonds.
MAKES 1¾ QUARTS.

Peach or Strawberry Ice Cream

This base is perfect for either fruit and easy to prepare in your electric ice cream maker.

2¾ cups heavy cream
1⅓ cups milk
1 teaspoon vanilla
7–8 egg yolks—7 if large, 8 if small
1 cup sugar plus 2 tablespoons
2¼ cups fresh peaches, diced, or strawberries, sliced
5 tablespoons sugar

Combine cream, milk, and vanilla in saucepan and bring to a boil. Cool. In an electric mixer combine yolks and sugar and beat until smooth. Slowly pour the hot cream mixture over the yolks stirring constantly on medium speed. Transfer all to the saucepan and cook the custard over low heat until thickened. Do not let boil. Pour into chilled bowl and refrigerate until cold.

Sprinkle the fruit of your choice with the 5 tablespoons sugar and fold into cold custard. Freeze in your electric freezer according to the manufacturer's instructions.
MAKES 2 QUARTS.

Strawberry Gin Ice Cream

4 cups fresh strawberries, puréed
1 cup sugar
½ cup dry gin
2 cups heavy cream
2 cups light cream
¼ teaspoon salt
Zest of 1 lemon

In a saucepan combine the strawberries, sugar, and gin and cook, stirring constantly, for 15 minutes. Cool completely, then add the balance of the ingredients. When blended, pour into ice cream freezer and freeze according to manufacturer's instructions.
MAKES 2½ QUARTS.

Pineapple Pistachio Ice Cream

When I was expecting my third child, I had a yen only for this—and only after midnight when all the stores were closed. My husband finally decided to keep the freezer well stocked!

8 egg yolks
1 cup sugar
½ cup ground unsalted
  pistachio nuts
1⅓ cups milk or half and half
2¾ cups heavy cream
1½ cups crushed pineapple,
  well drained
2–3 tablespoons pineapple
  juice

Beat the egg yolks with the sugar until smooth, add the nuts. Combine milk or half and half and cream in a saucepan and bring to a boil. Pour over the egg mixture, stirring and continuing to cook until the mixture almost reaches boiling and is thickened. Cool, add the crushed pineapple and pineapple juice. Freeze in ice cream freezer according to manufacturer's instructions.
MAKES 2 QUARTS.

Strawberry Sherbet

What could be better in the summer when strawberries are plentiful and at their best!

3 pints ripe strawberries
2 cups granulated sugar
Juice of 3 oranges, unstrained
Juice of 3 lemons, unstrained
6 tablespoons curaçao or
  Grand Marnier

Wash berries, drain well, then stem. Combine with the sugar, juices, and liqueur, and let stand at room temperature for 3–4 hours. Purée in blender and freeze.
MAKES 2 QUARTS.

Raspberry Sherry Mold

Because my mother and her helper for over nineteen years ruled the kitchen, I believe I was the only one of my married friends who had never learned to cook. This wonderful dessert recipe was given to me by Janet Emrich, a distant Linz relative and a superlative cook.

*10" springform, bottom and
    sides lightly buttered*
2 packages ladyfingers
1 cup plus 3 tablespoons sugar
1 cup milk
3 egg yolks, beaten
⅛ teaspoon nutmeg
Dash salt
1 envelope gelatin
*¼ cup plus 1 teaspoon sweet
    sherry*
¼ cup water
2 cups frozen raspberries
4 egg whites
1 cup heavy cream

Split the ladyfingers and line the bottom and sides of springform with them, split side facing in.

Dissolve the cup of sugar in the milk in the top of a double boiler over hot water.

Beat the yolks with the nutmeg and salt and pour in a steady stream into the hot milk mixture, stirring constantly. Remove from heat.

Dissolve gelatin in the ¼ cup sherry and water and add to yolk mixture. Mix well.

Pour custard into a blender, add frozen raspberries and purée. Strain to remove seeds, if you wish, and chill, stirring once in a while until custard begins to set. Beat egg whites and 2 tablespoons sugar to stiff peak and fold into chilled custard.

Whip cream with 1 tablespoon sugar and 1 teaspoon sherry. Lastly, fold the lightly sweetened whipped cream flavored with sherry into the chilled custard. Spoon into prepared springform and chill at least 2–3 hours.
SERVES 10.

VARIATION:
Instead of ladyfingers, use crumbled almond macaroons on the bottom and sides of the springform, saving some to dust the top.

Italian Cassata

This recipe came to me from my cousin Beatrice Kolliner in Los Angeles. I think it deserves publishing.

2 9" × 4" × 2" loaf pans,
  buttered
½ cup canned pineapple
  cubes, drained
½ cup candied cherries
½ cup candied orange peel or
  S&W-brand glazed mixed
  fruits
½ cup rum or brandy
1 pint rich vanilla ice cream
2 cups heavy cream, whipped
½ cup confectioners' sugar
2 teaspoons vanilla
1 pint rich chocolate ice cream

Soak the combined fruits in rum or brandy. Spread softened vanilla ice cream in pans to one-third of the depth. Freeze. Whip the heavy cream until stiff with the confectioners' sugar and vanilla, add brandied fruits, and spoon on top of vanilla ice cream to fill another third of each pan. Freeze. Soften chocolate ice cream and spread to fill the pans. Freeze. Unmold shortly before serving so it will not be freezer hard and difficult to slice at the table.

SERVES 8–10.

Sauces and Icings

Sauce Sabayon
Sauce Cerise
Vanilla Sauce
Praline-Toffee Sundae Sauce
Sauce Anglaise
Grand Marnier Sauce
Heavenly Hot Fudge Sauce
Confectioners' Chocolate Sauce
Confectioners' Dark Rum Sauce
Sissy Sauce
Sauce Tips
Tipsy Tips

§ ICINGS §
Devil's Icing
Chocolate Maple Frosting
Tipsy Orange Chocolate Icing
Chocolate Butter Frosting
Chocolate Butter Cream Frosting
Chocolate Divine Icing
Chocolate Cream Cheese Frosting
Old-Fashioned Penuche Icing

Sauce Sabayon

Delightful for fruit soufflés.

6 egg yolks
¾ cup sugar
Pinch salt
1 cup white wine, sherry, marsala, Madeira, or cognac

Beat the egg yolks until light and lemon colored in an electric mixer. Add sugar, salt, and wine, and blend well. Pour mixture into top of double boiler over hot, not boiling, water. Cook gently, beating constantly, until sauce is thick and foamy. Remove from heat and place in a bowl over ice. Continue beating until sauce is thoroughly cooled.
MAKES 2½ CUPS.

Sauce Cerise

A lovely combination of fruit with liqueur to be served over custards or ice cream.

1 10-ounce package frozen raspberries, thawed
1-pound can dark sweet cherries, pitted
1½ tablespoons sugar
1 tablespoon cornstarch
2½ tablespoons framboise (the red sweet) or cherry liqueur

Drain the fruits and reserve the liquids. Blend sugar and cornstarch in saucepan. Add the fruit juices slowly and cook, stirring constantly, until thickened. Add liqueur of your choice, taste for flavor, and reheat to remove alcohol. Cool, then add fruit.
MAKES ABOUT 2 CUPS.

Vanilla Sauce

Delicious served warm over fresh stewed peaches or pears.

2 egg yolks
1 egg
2 tablespoons sugar
½ cup Cointreau

Combine yolks and whole egg in top of double boiler over hot water. Beat with a rotary beater, add the sugar and beat, then slowly add the liqueur. Beat until light and thick.
MAKES 1½ CUPS.

Praline-Toffee Sundae Sauce

My thanks to the Praline liqueur people. This is truly worthy of a reprint!

¼ cup Praline liqueur
1 tablespoon instant coffee
Pinch salt
¼ cup water
1¼ cups brown sugar
1 can sweetened condensed milk
½ cup chopped pecans
1 teaspoon vanilla

Combine liqueur, coffee, salt, water, and sugar in heavy saucepan. Heat, stirring constantly, to a boil. Cook, without stirring, to 230°F on candy thermometer. Blend syrup slowly into the milk. Add pecans and vanilla. Serve over ice cream. Delish!
MAKES 3½ CUPS.

Sauce Anglaise

Delicious served cold over fresh fruit.

5 egg yolks
⅔ cup sugar
2 cups milk
Pinch salt
1½ tablespoons dark rum,
    kirschwasser, curaçao, or
    your choice of liqueur

Combine yolks and sugar in saucepan and beat until thick and light.

Bring milk just to a boil and gradually add to the yolk mixture, beating constantly with a wooden spoon. Cook over low heat, stirring constantly, add the salt, and continue to cook until custard coats the spoon. Never let the custard boil. Remove from heat, set in pan of cold water, and continue to stir. When cool, add the liqueur. Chill before serving.

MAKES ABOUT 3 CUPS.

Grand Marnier Sauce

Great over stewed fruit.

2 cups sugar
1 cup hot, extra-strong coffee
1 cup Grand Marnier
1 teaspoon vanilla

Melt the sugar in cast iron skillet over low heat until sugar is melted and a light brown. Remove from heat and slowly add the hot coffee, stirring constantly. Return to heat and cook over low heat until caramel is dissolved. Add liqueur and vanilla, and continue to cook, stirring, until slightly thickened. Serve hot.

MAKES 2½ CUPS.

Heavenly Hot Fudge Sauce

This sauce can be stored in the refrigerator and reheated many times. It is very smooth and just about the best I've ever tried.

4 squares bitter chocolate
1 stick butter or margarine
3 cups sugar
Pinch salt
1 large can evaporated milk

Melt chocolate and butter or margarine in top of a double boiler over simmering water. Add the sugar a little at a time, blending thoroughly after each addition. Add the salt and then gradually the evaporated milk. Remove from heat.

Serve hot over ice cream or puddings. Store the balance in refrigerator for another treat.
MAKES ABOUT 1 QUART.

Confectioners' Chocolate Sauce

This is a great base for the Confectioners' Dark Rum Sauce (p. 179) or the Sissy Sauce (p. 179) or just used alone. The addition of any liqueur, such as Kahlua or Amaretto, is a welcome touch. Try it plain first.

1 stick butter
2¼ cups confectioners' sugar, sifted
⅔ cup evaporated milk
6 squares bitter chocolate

Melt the butter and sugar in the top of a double boiler over low heat. Add the milk and chocolate and cook over hot water for 30 minutes, without stirring. Remove from the heat and beat. This sauce may be stored in the refrigerator and reheated over hot water as often as necessary. To thin the sauce, add only light or coffee cream.
MAKES 3 CUPS.

Confectioners' Dark Rum Sauce

Eat this with a spoon, serve it over ice cream or cake, or do both if you're underweight!

½ cup Confectioners' Chocolate Sauce (p. 178)
½ cup dark rum
1½ pints heavy cream, whipped

Melt chocolate sauce, add rum and cool completely. Fold in the whipped cream.
MAKES 3½ CUPS.

Sissy Sauce

This is devastating over rich vanilla ice cream or plain cake. You're a sissy if you don't try this!

1 cup Confectioners' Chocolate Sauce (p. 178)
¼ cup orange juice
2 tablespoons grated orange zest
2 teaspoons curaçao or Grand Marnier
Pinch salt

Heat the chocolate sauce and add the rest of the ingredients.
MAKES 1¼ CUPS.

Sauce Tips

Lemon (my favorite) or pineapple sherbet splashed with a tablespoon or two of sauterne is an excellent dessert after a heavy meal.

Coffee ice cream, softened enough to add Nestlés chocolate bits and/or the zest of orange rind can be refrozen and served as is, or softened to use as a sauce over vanilla ice cream. Or soften coffee ice cream, blend in dark rum, and serve over vanilla ice cream. It's great!

Chocolate ice cream doused with a tablespoon Cointreau or Triple Sec brings raves.

Homemade fresh peach ice cream splashed with apricot brandy and topped with toasted almonds is soul satisfying.

Vanilla ice cream softened with a few tablespoons of curaçao is divine over fresh strawberries, raspberries, or peaches.

Whipped cream (1 cup) blended with 2 teaspoons sugar, 1 teaspoon instant coffee, and 1 tablespoon crème de cacao will turn any plain pound cake into a regal dessert.

Tipsy Tips

Brandy with coffee.

Prunes soaked in brandy for about a week.

Bourbon marries well with chocolate mousse, so does rum.

Bourbon with peaches and dark brown sugar, dotted with butter and broiled!

Framboise with raspberries.

Kirschwasser with strawberries, apricots, or pineapple.

Match the liqueur to the fruit to double the decadence.

Aurum is a delightful, little-known liqueur from Italy. It has a wonderful orange flavor. I prefer it to others.

Applejack or calvados blends well with pineapple.

Rum adds vigor to chocolate, lemon, pineapple, and coffee.

ICING

One word about icings before I continue. Any chocolate candy—plain, bittersweet, milk, nut-filled, or otherwise—can be melted, in sufficient quantity, over hot water, and spread on cakes. About 1½ cups of melted candy will do.

Devil's Icing

½ cup brown sugar
½ cup water
2 tablespoons butter
2 squares bitter chocolate
2 cups confectioners' sugar
Pinch salt
1 teaspoon vanilla

In a sauce pan, boil brown sugar, water, and butter for a few minutes. Add chocolate. Remove from heat when chocolate has melted and add confectioners' sugar, salt, and vanilla. Beat until smooth and spreading consistency.
MAKES APPROXIMATELY 3 CUPS.

Chocolate Maple Frosting

Just a little bit different.

1½ ounces bitter chocolate
⅔ cup sweetened condensed
  milk
1 tablespoon cold water
½ teaspoon vanilla
1 teaspoon maple flavoring

Melt the chocolate in top of double boiler over simmering water. Add milk and cook 5 minutes, stirring constantly, until thick. Add water and flavoring. Continue cooking and stirring until right consistency for spreading.
MAKES APPROXIMATELY 1¼ CUPS.

Tipsy Orange Chocolate Icing

Here's something special to perk up a plain chocolate cake.

3 cups confectioners' sugar
½ cup grated dark sweet chocolate
2–3 tablespoons cream
4–5 tablespoons butter
2 tablespoons strong black
   coffee
2 tablespoons orange juice
2 tablespoons brandy

Sift sugar. Add all ingredients together and blend in a double boiler over hot water. Add more cream, if necessary, to thin. Or increase the amount of brandy.

MAKES APPROXIMATELY 3½ CUPS.

Chocolate Butter Frosting

2 squares bitter chocolate
3 tablespoons butter
¼ cup heavy cream
Pinch salt
1 teaspoon vanilla or rum or
   sherry
2 cups sifted confectioners'
   sugar

Combine chocolate and butter in double boiler and heat over simmering water until chocolate is melted. Warm cream and add to the chocolate with salt. Cool. Add flavoring and sugar gradually. Beat until smooth and right consistency for spreading.

WILL ICE 2 8-INCH LAYERS (APPROXIMATELY 3 CUPS).

Chocolate Butter Cream Frosting

6 ounces semisweet chocolate
   morsels
1 stick butter, softened
1 egg yolk, beaten
2 teaspoons brandy
½ teaspoon vanilla
2 tablespoons confectioners'
   sugar
Toasted slivered almonds for
   garnish

Melt the chocolate morsels in the top of a double boiler over simmering water. Remove from heat.

Cream the butter, add melted chocolate, blend well, then add the other ingredients. Spread over cake. Decorate top of cake with toasted slivered almonds.

YIELD: SUFFICIENT TO COVER A 10″ TUBE CAKE OR A 9″ LAYER CAKE.

Chocolate Divine Icing

2 cups dark brown sugar,
  firmly packed
8 ounces bitter chocolate
2 tablespoons light corn syrup
¾ cup light cream
2 tablespoons butter
2 teaspoons vanilla
Pinch salt

Combine sugar, chocolate, syrup, and cream in saucepan and stir over low heat until sugar is dissolved. Cook without stirring until soft-ball stage has been reached, 238°F on candy thermometer. Remove from heat and add butter. Cool the icing over ice water, then add vanilla. Beat until right consistency to spread.
WILL FILL AND FROST A 2 LAYER 9-INCH CAKE (APPROXIMATELY 4 CUPS).

Chocolate Cream Cheese Frosting

2 3-ounce packages cream
  cheese
4 tablespoons milk
4 cups confectioners' sugar,
  sifted
4½ squares bitter chocolate,
  melted
Pinch salt
1 teaspoon vanilla

Mix cheese with milk, add sugar, and beat well. Mix in melted chocolate, salt, and vanilla.
THIS WILL ICE 2 8-INCH LAYERS (APPROXIMATELY 3 CUPS).

Old-Fashioned Penuche Icing

2 cups light brown sugar,
  firmly packed
½ cup milk
1 stick butter
¼ teaspoon salt
1¼ teaspoons vanilla
½ cup chopped pecans

Blend the first four ingredients together in a saucepan over low heat until thoroughly melted. Increase heat and bring to a boil for 1 minute, stirring constantly. Remove from heat and continue to beat until cool and of desired consistency for spreading. Add flavoring and chopped pecans.
MAKES APPROXIMATELY 3 CUPS.

Candies and Confections

Lazy Day Chocolate Butterscotch Bars
Bittersweet Chocolate Hash
Chocolate-Covered Marshmallows and Fruit Peel
Chocolate Coconut Drops
Chocolate Fondue
Chocolate Fruit Confections
Chocolate Nut Tartlets
Chocolate Orange Turtles
Chocolate Rum Caramels
Chocolate Swirls
Black Walnut Drops
Coconut Raisin Drops
Dr. Pepper Pralines
Chocolate Candy Cups
Oriental Poppies

Lazy Day Chocolate Butterscotch Bars

A can't-miss recipe, even for a brand-new bride.

9" × 12" pan
½ stick butter, melted
1 cup honey graham cracker
  crumbs
1 3½-ounce can flaked
  coconut
6 ounces semisweet chocolate
  morsels
6 ounces butterscotch morsels
15-ounce can sweetened
  condensed milk
½ teaspoon vanilla
1 cup chopped pecans

Preheat oven to 350°F.
  Combine the melted butter with the crumbs and press into the pan. Add each ingredient evenly in the order in which they are listed. Bake in preheated oven for 20–25 minutes. Cool in pan and cut into squares.
YIELD: 16 SQUARES.

Bittersweet Chocolate Hash

A nice addition for a sweet table.

8" square pan, buttered
1 small package miniature
  marshmallows
1 cup chopped nuts, either
  pecans or slivered toasted
  almonds, or a blend of
  both
½ cup candied cherries,
  halved
¼ pound dark sweet chocolate
½ pound bitter chocolate

Combine marshmallows, nuts, and cherries in a bowl. Melt both chocolates in the top of a double boiler over hot water. Cool slightly, and pour over nut mixture. Mix well and spoon into prepared pan. When cool cut in small squares and place in candy wrapper cups.
MAKES 20–25 SQUARES.

Chocolate-Covered Marshmallows and Fruit Peel

The amount of chocolate needed depends solely on the amount of marsh-mallows or fruit to be dipped. This is another nice addition to a sweet table.

Drained maraschino cherries and pitted dates may be treated the same way.

Prepared orange and grape-
    fruit peel
4–6 ounces dark sweet choco-
    late
Large marshmallows

To prepare fruit peel, discard all white pith and cut peel in ¼ inch strips. For every orange or grapefruit, combine ½ cup granulated sugar with ¼ cup water. Bring the syrup to a boil, then add the peel and cook until the syrup is nearly evapo-rated. Drain on waxed paper and cool.

Melt chocolate in top of double boiler over hot water. Dip marshmallows and fruit strips in choc-olate and cool on waxed paper.

Chocolate Coconut Drops

Baking sheet, greased
½ cup shortening
½ cup sugar
½ cup packed dark brown
    sugar
1 egg
1½ cups flour
½ teaspoon baking powder
¼ teaspoon salt
1 7-ounce bar semisweet
    chocolate
½ cup moist shredded un-
    sweetened coconut

Preheat oven to 375°F.

Cream shortening and sugars together. Beat egg and add. Sift together the flour, baking powder, and salt, and add. Chop chocolate; add with coconut. Mix well. Drop by teaspoons on greased baking sheet and bake for 10 minutes.
MAKES ABOUT 3 DOZEN.

Chocolate Fondue

A perfect ending for a buffet dinner. The sauce can double as a topping for vanilla ice cream.

For fondue, the essentials are pineapple chunks—preferably fresh—toothpicks, and a chafing dish. Candied fruits, especially cherries, are also good. Place a toothpick in each piece of fruit; place on foil, and freeze. Guests dip each piece of frozen fruit into the hot chocolate. The chocolate congeals and the fruit defrosts slightly. Delicious!

4 cups brown sugar
1⅓ cups milk
1 stick butter
4½ ounces semisweet chocolate
4 tablespoons crème de cacao
4 tablespoons cognac

Combine all ingredients except liqueurs in a saucepan over low heat, and stir until melted and well blended. Add the liqueurs and transfer to heated chafing dish. Keep warm but do not cook. Surround the platter with the frozen fruits.
MAKES APPROXIMATELY 6 CUPS.

Chocolate Fruit Confections

1 cup semisweet chocolate pieces
½ cup sour cream
½ pound vanilla wafers
Confectioners' sugar
¼ teaspoon salt
3 tablespoons cocoa
1 tablespoon grated lemon rind
1 tablespoon grated orange rind
2½ tablespoons lemon juice
1½ tablespoons maple syrup
¼ cup rum
1 cup finely chopped pecans

Melt chocolate over hot water and cool. Add cream and refrigerate overnight. Using ½ teaspoon of mixture for each, form into 54 balls. (These are the centers.)

Crush wafers. Add 1 cup sugar, salt, cocoa, and fruit rinds. Blend in lemon juice, syrup, rum, and pecans. Shape around the chocolate centers until you form balls the size of walnuts. Roll in powdered sugar. Store in airtight containers. Can be frozen.
MAKES 4½ DOZEN.

Chocolate Nut Tartlets

A perfect end for a dinner party. These are spectacular on a buffet table.

24 muffin tins, greased
⅔ cup sugar
6 tablespoons all-purpose flour
1 egg white, kept aside
1⅓ cups ground almonds
3 ounces semisweet chocolate, grated
2 tablespoons confectioners' sugar
4 teaspoons hot water
5–6 tablespoons butter
2 eggs, separated
¼ cup toasted sliced almonds for garnish

Preheat oven to 300°F.

Combine sugar, flour, 1 egg white, and ground almonds, and work into a dough. Roll on floured board about ⅛ inch thick. Cut in circles and line muffin tins. Bake in oven 20 minutes, until lightly browned. Cool before removing from tins.

Combine chocolate, confectioners' sugar, and 4 teaspoons hot water in top of double boiler; stir over low heat until melted. Remove from heat and add butter and yolks, and beat with electric mixer 15 minutes. Beat remaining 2 egg whites until stiff, fold into chocolate mixture, and beat another 15 minutes. Fill baked shells and chill overnight. Garnish with toasted almonds. YIELDS 24.

Chocolate Orange Turtles

This delicacy tops the list for favorites. Years ago, one of the best cooks in Dallas, who was a dear friend of the family, baked these. On special occasions, we would receive a box of these goodies.

Cookie sheet, greased and floured
4 ounces dark sweet chocolate
½ cup heavy cream
3–4 tablespoons sugar
Pinch salt
¾–1 cup chopped preserved orange rind
½ cup chopped almonds
¼ cup all-purpose flour

Preheat oven to 350°F.

Over hot water, melt chocolate and set aside. Combine cream with all other ingredients and drop mixture from teaspoon on greased and floured cookie sheet. Bake in preheated oven for 8–10 minutes. These are very thin. Let cool, then turn over and coat bottom with melted chocolate. Let dry thoroughly, then serve. MAKES 3½–4 DOZEN.

Chocolate Rum Caramels

8" square pan, buttered
2 cups sugar
1 cup packed dark brown
   sugar
1 cup dark corn syrup
½ cup cream, light or heavy
Pinch salt
3½ ounces bitter chocolate
1 stick butter
1 teaspoon rum
¾ cup chopped pecans

Combine all ingredients, except rum and nuts, in saucepan; cover and boil for 5–6 minutes. Uncover and cook to hard-ball stage, 247°F on candy thermometer. Remove from heat, add rum and nuts, and pour into pan. Cool. When cold, cut into squares and wrap in waxed paper.
MAKES ABOUT 4½ DOZEN PIECES.

Chocolate Swirls

Children love these.

Muffin tins, buttered
1 stick butter
1½ cups sugar
3 eggs
2 cups flour
4 teaspoons baking powder
¼ teaspoon salt
½ cup milk
1 teaspoon vanilla
2 tablespoons cocoa

Preheat oven to 375°F.
   Cream butter with sugar, then beat in eggs one at a time.
   Sift flour, baking powder, and salt together and add alternately with milk to butter mixture. Add vanilla. Divide batter into two equal parts; add cocoa to one. Put one spoon of dark and one of white batter into each muffin tin. Bake for 15–20 minutes. Frost with any good chocolate icing.
YIELDS 24.

Black Walnut Drops

Keep these drops refrigerated to keep them fresh.

Cookie sheet, buttered and
  floured
1 egg
Pinch salt
½ cup dark brown sugar,
  packed
3 tablespoons all-purpose
  flour
½ cup chopped walnuts
3 ounces sweet chocolate
1 tablespoon butter

Preheat oven to 400°F.
　　Beat the egg with the salt, add the sugar and beat until thick. Mix in the flour and chopped walnuts. Blend well, then drop by teaspoonfuls onto prepared cookie sheet. Bake for 6–8 minutes. Cool on pan.
　　In a double boiler over simmering water, melt the chocolate with the butter, then brush the top of each drop with the mixture. Chill.
YIELD: 36 DROPS.

Coconut Raisin Drops

I am allergic to coconut so I haven't tasted these, but my family loved them.

Cookie sheet, buttered and
  floured
12 tablespoons butter
¾ cup sugar
1 egg, beaten
1½ teaspoons lemon zest
2 cups all-purpose flour, sifted
Pinch salt
1 cup flaked coconut
½ cup raisins
¼ cup chopped walnuts

Preheat oven to 400°F.
　　Blend butter and sugar until light. Add beaten egg and zest. Add balance of ingredients, mix thoroughly and drop by tablespoonfuls onto prepared cookie sheet. Bake for 20 minutes, until lightly browned.
YIELD: ABOUT 36 DROPS.

Dr. Pepper Pralines

This is certainly a departure from the southern praline as we know it. The Dr. Pepper kitchens devised these and they are delicious.

1 cup sugar
1 cup dark brown sugar, packed
1 cup Dr. Pepper soda
4 large marshmallows
2½ cups pecan halves

In a heavy saucepan, mix together both sugars with the Dr. Pepper. Cook over low heat, stirring constantly until all sugar is dissolved; then cook, stirring occasionally until the soft-ball stage (238°F) is reached. Remove from heat, add marshmallows and pecans. Beat vigorously 1–2 minutes until mixture is creamy. Drop on waxed paper in small balls, about 1 tablespoon at a time. They should flatten out around the edges, leaving a mound of pecans in center. After removing from heat, work fast as candy sets up quickly.
MAKES ABOUT 30 LARGE PATTIES.

Chocolate Candy Cups

These are always a success at children's birthday parties.

6 ounces semisweet chocolate bits
2 tablespoons butter

Melt chocolate and butter together over hot water and pour into small paper baking cups, spreading with the back of a teaspoon to cover the sides. Set in muffin tins and chill. Fill with ice cream or any butter filling. Sprinkle tops with ground nuts or chocolate bits.
MAKES 12.

Oriental Poppies

As I recall, Friday at Grandmother's house was a wonderful day full of tempting aromas from the kitchen. No one was allowed into her sanctum sanctorum until about four in the afternoon, when the day's preparation for the Sabbath was nearly over. Then we—me and the neighborhood children—were there begging for samples. As Grandmother was one who never measured, this is as near as I can come to one of her goodies.

Cookie sheet, buttered
1 stick butter
½ cup sugar
¾ cup poppy seeds
½ cup hot milk
1¼ cups flour
1 teaspoon baking powder
½ teaspoon cinnamon
Pinch salt
¼ teaspoon vanilla
3 ounces dark sweet chocolate, grated
¾ cup currants or white raisins
Confectioners' sugar, sifted, for garnish

Preheat oven to 350°F.
Combine butter with sugar, and cream until light. Soak poppy seeds in hot milk for 5 minutes. Sift flour with all dry ingredients and add to butter mixture alternately with poppy seeds and milk. Add rest of ingredients and drop teaspoonfuls onto cookie sheet. Bake for 15–20 minutes. Cool on rack. Dust with sifted confectioners' sugar when cold.
MAKES 3½ DOZEN.

Beverages

Café Sabayon
Tia Maria Frappé
Father's Eggnog
Black Coffee Eggnog
Málaga Scotched Coffee
Debbie's Brandied Coffee
Frapped Café de Cacao
Iced Café
Dessert Café
Café Orange
Iced Coffee Tip

Café Sabayon

I'm a twangy Texan who grew up on straight drinks, and to this day, I prefer it that way. But some of my guests don't, and to please, I added a few of these delights to my repertory.

6 egg yolks
½ cup sugar
4 tablespoons Grand Marnier
2 tablespoons extra-strong coffee, espresso if you have it
2 tablespoons lemon juice

In the top of a double boiler over simmering water, beat all the ingredients until blended. Beat with a wire whisk over boiling water only until custard begins to thicken. Spoon into dessert glasses. Serve warm or cold.
SERVES 4–5.

Tia Maria Frappé

You will find this to be a lovely drink, summer or winter.

1 quart rich vanilla ice cream, softened
6 tablespoons Amaretto liqueur
5 tablespoons Tia Maria or Kahlua
2 tablespoons Triple Sec
Lightly sweetened whipped cream for garnish

Combine all in a bowl and blend until smooth. Keep chilled in refrigerator until ready to serve, then spoon into tall frosty glasses, topped with lightly sweetened whipped cream.
SERVES 6–8.

Father's Eggnog

In our family we always served this delight on Christmas Day—but not just because of the holiday. It was Mother's birthday, and the entire family and our friends came to our annual open house to help celebrate. Father devised this eggnog to add to the general good cheer, and it certainly did—after a cup or two of this brew, all was well with the world.

1 dozen eggs, separated
¾ cup sugar
¾ cup bourbon whiskey
½ cup dark rum
1 pint heavy cream, whipped
Nutmeg for garnish

Beat the egg yolks until they are light and lemon colored. Add the sugar and blend well. Add the bourbon and rum, and continue to beat until well blended.

Half an hour before serving, whip the egg whites to a peak and fold them into the mixture. Chill.

Whip the cream, fold it into the mixture, and chill again briefly. Serve the eggnog with a ladle from a large chilled tureen. Dust each cupful with nutmeg.
SERVES ABOUT 15.

Black Coffee Eggnog

This eggnog is not as thick as Father's, but it is certainly unique and delicious.

1 dozen eggs, separated
1 cup sugar
2 cups light rum
2 cups cold, extra-strength coffee (espresso, if you can)
6 cups light cream
Nutmeg for garnish

Beat the yolks until they are light and lemon colored. Add the sugar and blend well. Add the rum, coffee, and the cream. Refrigerate.

Beat the egg whites to a peak and fold into the nog mixture. Chill.

Dust each cupful with nutmeg before serving.
SERVES ABOUT 12–15.

Málaga Scotched Coffee

In August 1974 my husband, Guy, daughter, Deborah, and I, traveled to Spain. Our first stop was Málaga and it's being lunchtime we stopped at a seaside open-air restaurant named Antonio Martins. After stuffing ourselves on lobster, funny hairy crabs, and native barnacles and wine, we saw a tall dessert flash by to another table. Debbie and I each ordered one. There is nothing like being smashed in the middle of the afternoon when the temperature is 110°F and the afternoon itinerary includes a climb up the mountain to the Alcazaba Tower and Museum! Try this in the wintertime.

Ice tea glass or ice cream soda
glass
Extra-strong coffee, cold
1½ ounces White Horse
scotch—this is the only
scotch in Spain and the
only scotch to use
1 scoop vanilla ice cream
1 dollop whipped cream

Pour cold coffee and scotch into chilled glass, being sure to leave room for ice cream. Stir. Add ice cream and top with whipped cream. SERVES 1.

Debbie's Brandied Coffee

After three years of college, you would have thought she'd know better—but she didn't! All my brandy glasses were destroyed. But to say it wasn't worth it would be a lie. My advice would be to use flameproof brandy snifters. It's divine!

As it was given to me by Debbie, per person.

1 tablespoon brandy
⅓ cup extra-strong coffee
⅓ cup Tia Maria
1 teaspoon Amaretto
Sweetened whipped cream
Brandied cherries

Pour brandy into snifter, ignite, rotate glass, and let burn out. Add coffee and liqueurs and blend. Top with whipped cream and cherries. SERVES 1.

Frappéed Café de Cacao

A delicious blending for coffee lovers.

½ cup extra-strong, cold
  coffee
½ cup crushed ice
6 tablespoons crème de cacao
1 teaspoon white crème de
  menthe
1 large scoop vanilla ice cream

Combine all in a blender until ice is crushed.
SERVES 4.

Iced Café

This is delicious any time of the year, but particularly welcome in the summer as an afternoon pick-me-up.

8 scoops coffee ice cream
¼ cup chocolate syrup
¼ cup extra-strong, cold coffee—regular or espresso
¼ cup cognac or brandy
Bittersweet chocolate for
  garnish

Place all ingredients except chocolate in electric blender and mix on low only until blended. Serve in ice tea glasses with grated bittersweet chocolate.
SERVES 4.

Dessert Café

This potable can double for dessert and beverage after dinner.

6 teaspoons sugar
2 small sticks of cinnamon,
  cracked
6 whole cloves
Rind of half an orange
Rind of half a lemon
½ cup brandy
4 cups extra-strong fresh coffee, piping hot

Place all ingredients, except the coffee, in chafing dish. Heat and stir until all the sugar is dissolved and liquid is hot. Flambé the brandy. When the blue flame is out, add the coffee, blend all, and spoon into demitasse cups.
SERVES 6.

Café Orange

Instead of an after-dinner drink with coffee, try this blending.

For each demitasse cup, fill two-thirds with espresso, then add Grand Marnier to the top.

Iced Coffee Tip

Freeze leftover coffee in ice cube trays. Keep collecting it and use the cubes for iced coffee, instead of ice cubes that will dilute the strength of the drink.

Index